This new edition published 2004 by Lexus Ltd
60 Brook Street, Glasgow G40 2AB
Maps drawn by András Bereznay
Typeset by Elfreda Crehan
Series editor: Peter Terrell

First published in 1982 by Richard Drew Publishing Ltd,
ISBN 0-904002-75-6
Published in 1991 by W & R Chambers Ltd, ISBN 0-550-
22001-1

British Library Cataloguing in Publication Data
A catalogue record for this book is available from the
British Library.

ISBN 1-904737-01-3

Printed and bound in Great Britain by Scotprint

Your Travelmate

gives you one single easy-to-use A to Z list of words and phrases to help you communicate in French.

Built into this list are:

- travel tips (✈) with facts and figures which provide valuable information
- French words you'll see on signs and notices
- typical replies to some of the things you might want to say
- language notes giving you basic information about speaking the language
- a menu reader on pages 84-87

There are maps of France, Belgium and Switzerland on pages 155-158. Numbers and the French alphabet are on pages 159-160.

Speaking French

Your Travelmate also tells you how to pronounce French. Just read the pronunciation guides given in square brackets as though they were English and you will communicate – although you might not sound exactly like a native speaker.

If no pronunciation is given this is because the French word itself can be spoken more or less as though it were English.

In a very few cases where the French translation is in fact an English word then this translation is put in quotes.

Sometimes only a part of a word or phrase needs a pronunciation guide.

Stress

Give equal weight to all the syllables in a word when speaking French.

Some special points about the pronunciation system used to represent French:

ah	like the a in f**a**ther
air	like the air sound in h**air**
AN	a nasal sound, say the a as in v**a**n but don't pronounce the n
ay	like the ay in p**ay**, but shorter
eh	like the e in l**e**ss
g, gh	like the g in **g**o
I	like the i in h**i**
J	like the s in plea**s**ure or the z in sei**z**ure
ON	a nasal sound, say the o sound as in R**o**n, but don't pronounce the n
oo	like the oo in b**oo**t
∞	like the ew in f**ew**, without any 'y' sound
uh	like the u in b**u**tter

Men and women speaking

When you see an entry with a slash like:

I'm not ready yet je ne suis pas encore prêt/prête [Juh nuh swee pa zON-kor preh/pret]

the French given after the slash is the form to be used by female speakers. So a man would say:

I'm not ready yet je ne suis pas encore prêt [Juh nuh swee pa zON-kor preh]

and a woman would say:

I'm not ready yet je ne suis pas encore prête [Juh nuh swee pa zON-kor pret]

Similarly, when two translations are given, as in:

cool frais/fraîche [freh/fresh]

the first translation is for use with masculine nouns (with **un** or **le**) and the second with feminine nouns (with **une** or **la**).

Language backup

To find out more about Lexus and Lexus Translations or to comment on this book you can go on-line to www.lexusforlanguages.co.uk.

A [ah]

a, an un/une [AN/ɶn]

> **Un** and **une** correspond to the words for 'the' **le** and **la**.

about: is he about? est-ce qu'il est là? [eskeeleh la]

  about 15 environ quinze [ONvee-rON kANz]

  about 2 o'clock vers deux heures [vair...]

above au-dessus [o duh-sɶ]

  above the village au-dessus du village

abroad à l'étranger [ah laytrON-Jay]

absolutely! tout à fait! [toota feh]

accelerator l'accélérateur [axay-lay-ra-tur]

accept accepter [axeptay]

accès interdit no entry

accueil reception

accident un accident [axee-dON]

  there's been an accident il y a eu un accident [eelya ɶ...]

> ✈ For accidents, make sure both parties sign the **constat à l'amiable** or **constat européen d'accident** (forms provided with your green card documents).

accotements non stabilisés soft verges

accurate précis [pray-see]

across: across the street *de l'autre côté de* la rue [duh lohtr ko-tay duh...]

adaptor un adaptateur [adapta-tur]

address une adresse [ad-ress]

  will you give me your address? est-ce que vous pouvez me donner votre adresse? [eskuh voo poovay muh donay...]

adjust ajuster [aJɶstay]

admission l'entrée [ON-tray]

advance: can we book in advance? est-ce qu'on peut réserver *à l'avance*? [eskON puh rayzair-vay ah la-vONss]

advert une annonce [a-nONss]

afraid: I'm afraid so eh oui [eh wee]
   I'm afraid not malheureusement pas [malur-rurzmON pa]

after après [apreh]
   after you après vous [...voo]

afternoon l'après-midi [apreh-mee-dee]
   in the afternoon l'après-midi
   this afternoon cet après-midi

aftershave un après-rasage [apreh-ra-zahJ]

again encore [ONkor]

against contre [kONtr]

age l'âge [ahJ]
   under age mineur [mee-nur]
   it takes ages ça met très longtemps [sa meh treh lON-tON]

ago: a week ago il y a une semaine [eelya...]
   it wasn't long ago il n'y a pas longtemps [eel n-ya pa lON-tON]
   how long ago was that? il y a combien de temps? [eelya kONb-yAN...]

agree: I agree je suis d'accord [Juh swee da-kor]
   it doesn't agree with me ça ne me réussit pas [sanmuh ray-oosee pa]

air l'air
   by air en avion [ON nav-yON]

air-conditioning: with air-conditioning climatisé [kleema-tee-zay]

air hostess l'hôtesse de l'air

airmail: by airmail par avion [...av-yON]

airport l'aéroport [ah-ayro-por]

airport bus la navette de l'aéroport [navet duh la-ayro-por]

aisle seat une place côté couloir [plass ko-tay kool-wahr]

alarm clock le réveil [ray-vay]

alcohol l'alcool [al-kol]

  is it alcoholic? est-ce que c'est alcoolisé? [eskuh seh alkolee-zay]

alimentation food

alive: is he still alive? est-ce qu'il est encore vivant? [eskeeleh ONkor veevON]

all tout [too]

  that's all c'est tout [seh...]

  all night toute la nuit [toot...]

  all the flights tous les vols [too...]

  all I have tout ce que j'ai [tooskuh...]

  thank you – not at all merci – de rien [mairsee duh ree-yAN]

all right d'accord [da-kor]

  it's all right ça va [sa...]

  I'm all right ça va

allergic: I'm allergic to... je suis allergique à... [Juh swee zalair-Jeek ah]

allowed: is it allowed? est-ce que c'est *permis*? [eskuh seh pairmee]

  allow me permettez-moi [pairmetay mwa]

allumez vos phares switch your headlights on

almost presque [presk]

alone seul [surl]

  did you come here alone? est-ce que vous êtes venu ici tout seul/toute seule? [eskuh voo zet vuh-nœ ee-see too surl/toot surl]

  leave me alone laissez-moi tranquille [lessay mwa trON-keel]

Alps: the Alps les Alpes [alp]

already déjà [day-Ja]

also aussi [o-see]

although bien que [b-yAN kuh]

altogether ensemble [ON-sONbl]

what does that make altogether? qu'est-ce que ça fait au total? [keskuh sa feh o toh-tal]

always toujours [tooJOOR]

am¹ *(in the morning)* du matin [...dœ matAN]

✈ The 24-hour system is commonly used in spoken French.

am² go to **be**

ambulance une ambulance [ONbœ-lONss]

get an ambulance! appelez une ambulance! [aplay...]

✈ Dial 15 for the SAMU.

America l'Amérique [amay-reek]

American *(adjective)* américain [amay-ree-kAN]
(man) un Américain
(woman) une Américaine [amay-ree-ken]

among parmi [parmee]

amp: a 13 amp fuse un fusible de 13 ampères [fœzeebl duh...ONpair]

anchor l'ancre [ONkr]

and et [ay]

angry fâché [fashay]

I'm very angry (about it) je suis furieux/ furieuse [Juh swee fœoree-uh/fœoree-urz]

ankle la cheville [shuh-vee-yuh]

anniversary: it's our anniversary c'est notre anniversaire de mariage [seh notr anee-vair-sair duh mar-yahJ]

annoy: he's annoying me il m'embête [eel mONbet]

it's very annoying c'est très ennuyeux [seh treh zON-nwee-yuh]

anorak un anorak

another: can we have another room? est-ce qu'on peut avoir *une autre* chambre? [eskON puh avwahr œn ohtr...]

another beer, please une autre bière, s'il vous plaît

answer la réponse [ray-pONss]

what was his answer? qu'est-ce qu'il a répondu? [keskeela raypONdoo]

there was no answer ça ne répondait pas [sa nuh raypONday pa]

antibiotics des antibiotiques [ONtee-bee-oteek]

antifreeze l'antigel [ONtee-Jel]

any: have you got any bananas/butter? est-ce que vous avez *des* bananes/*du* beurre? [eskuh voo zavay day.../doo...]

we haven't got any money/tickets nous n'avons pas d'argent/de billets [noo navON pa darJON/duh bee-yeh]

I haven't got any je n'en ai pas [Juh nON nay pa]

anybody: is anybody here? est-ce qu'il y a *quelqu'un*? [eskeelya kelkAN]

we don't know anybody here nous ne connaissons *personne* ici [...pair-son...]

anything: have you got anything for...? est-ce que vous avez *quelque chose* pour...? [eskuh voo zavay kelkuh shohz poor]

I don't want anything je n'ai besoin de *rien* [Juh nay buh-zwAN duh ree-yAN]

apology: please accept my apologies je vous prie de m'excuser [Juh voo pree duh mexkoo-zay]

appellation contrôlée quality label, guarantee that a wine comes from a particular area

appendicitis l'appendicite [apAN-dee-seet]

appetite l'appétit [apay-tee]

I've lost my appetite j'ai perdu l'appétit [Jay pairdoo...]

apple une pomme [pom]

apple pie une tarte aux pommes [tart o pom]

appointment: can I make an appointment? est-

ce que je peux prendre *rendez-vous*? [eskuh JUH
puh proNdr roNday-voo]

appuyer push
apricot un abricot [abreeko]
April avril [a-vreel]
aqualung une bouteille d'oxygène [bootay
doxeeJen]
are *go to* **be**
area *(neighbourhood)* la région [rayJ-yoN]
area code l'indicatif [ANdee-ka-teef]

> ✈ If you're in France (or Belgium or
> Switzerland) you need to include the zero
> of the area code. But not if calling from
> abroad.

arm le bras [bra]
around *go to* **about**
arrange: will you arrange it? est-ce que vous
pouvez vous en occuper? [eskuh voo poovay voo
zoN okoo-pay]
arrest *(verb)* arrêter [aray-tay]
arrêt stop
arrival l'arrivée [aree-vay]
arrive arriver [aree-vay]
  we only arrived yesterday nous ne sommes
  arrivés qu'hier [noo nuh som aree-vay k-yair]
art l'art [ar]
art gallery un musée d'art [moo-zay dar]
  (private) une galerie d'art [galuh-ree...]
arthritis l'arthrite [ar-treet]
artificial artificiel [artee-feess-yel]
artist un/une artiste [ar-teest]
as: as quickly as you can aussi vite que possible
  [o-see veet kuh posseebl]
  as much as you can autant que vous pouvez
  [o-toN kuh voo poovay]
  as you like comme vous voulez [kom voo voolay]

ascenseur lift
ashore à terre [ah tair]
  to go ashore débarquer [day-barkay]
ashtray un cendrier [sONdree-yay]
ask demander [duhmON-day]
  could you ask him to...? est-ce que vous
  pouvez lui demander de...? [eskuh voo poovay
  lwee...]
  that's not what I asked for ce n'est pas ce que
  j'ai demandé [suh neh pa suh kuh Jay duhmON-day]
asleep: he's still asleep il dort encore [eel dor
  ONkor]
asparagus des asperges [aspairJ]
aspirin une aspirine [aspee-reen]
assistant *(in shop)* le vendeur [VON-dur]
  (woman) la vendeuse [VON-durz]
asthma l'asthme [ass-muh]
at à [ah]
  at Sophie's chez Sophie [shay...]

> When **à** is used with **le** it becomes **au**.
> With the plural **les** it becomes **aux**.
>   **at the café** au café [o...]

attitude l'attitude
attractive: I think you're very attractive *(to
man/woman)* je vous trouve très beau/belle [Juh
voo troov treh bo/bel]
aubergine une aubergine [o-bair-Jeen]
August août [oot]
aunt: my aunt ma tante [...tONt]
Australia l'Australie [ostra-lee]
Australian australien/australienne [ostral-yAN/
ostral-yen]
Austria l'Autriche [o-treesh]
authorities les autorités [otoreetay]
automatic automatique [otomateek]
  (car) une automatique

autumn: in the autumn en automne [ON oton]
away: is it far away from here? est-ce que c'est
  loin d'ici? [eskuh seh lwAN dee-see]
  go away! allez-vous en! [alay voo zON]
awful affreux [a-fruh]
axle l'essieu [ess-yuh]

B [bay]

baby un bébé [baybay]
  we'd like a baby-sitter nous cherchons un/une
  baby-sitter [noo shair-shON...]
back (of body) le dos [doh]
  I've got a bad back j'ai un problème de dos
  [Jay AN prob-lem duh...]
  at the back derrière [dair-yair]
  I'll be right back je reviens tout de suite [Juh
  ruhv-yAN toot sweet]
  is he back? est-ce qu'il est revenu? [eskeeleh
  ruh-vuhnoo]
  can I have my money back? est-ce que vous
  pouvez me rendre mon argent? [eskuh voo
  poovay muh rONdr...]
  I go back tomorrow je rentre demain [Juh
  rONtr duh-mAN]
backpacker le randonneur [rONdonur]
  (female) la randonneuse [rONdonurz]
bacon le bacon [baykon]
  bacon and eggs des œufs au bacon [day zuh
  o...]
bad mauvais [mo-veh]
  it's not bad c'est pas mal [seh pa...]
  too bad! tant pis! [tON pee]
bag un sac [sak]
  (suitcase) une valise [valeez]
  (handbag) un sac à main [...ah mAN]
baggage les bagages [bagahJ]

baignade interdite no bathing

baker's une boulangerie [boolONJ-ree]

balcony un balcon [bal-kON]
a room with a balcony une chambre avec balcon [oon shONbr...]

bald chauve [shohv]

ball *(football etc)* un ballon [ba-lON]
(tennis, golf) une balle [bal]

ball-point (pen) un stylo à bille [steelo ah bee]

banana une banane [ba-nan]

band *(musical)* un orchestre [or-kestr]
(pop) un groupe [groop]

bandage le bandage [bON-dahJ]
could you change the bandage? est-ce que vous pouvez changer le bandage? [eskuh voo poovay shONJay...]

bank *(for money)* une banque [bONk]

> ✈ Open 9am-5pm in large towns Mon-Fri and 9-12 Sat. morning. May close earlier or between 12 and 2pm in smaller towns.

bank holiday *go to* **public holiday**

bar un bar
in the bar au bar [o...]

> ✈ If you sit at a table, the waiter will come and take your order. You pay when you leave.

> *YOU MAY HEAR*
> vous désirez? *what can I get you?*

barber's le coiffeur pour hommes [kwa-fur poor om]

bargain: it's a real bargain c'est une bonne affaire [set oon bon afair]

barmaid la serveuse [sair-vurz]

barman le 'barman'

baseball cap une casquette de 'base-ball'
[kasket...]
basket un panier [pan-yay]
bath un bain [bAN]
  (tub) la baignoire [ben-ywahr]
  can I have a bath? est-ce que je peux prendre
  un bain? [eskuh Juh puh proNdr AN bAN]
  could you give me a bath towel? est-ce que
  vous pouvez me donner *une serviette de bain*?
  [eskuh voo poovay muh donay con sairv-yet...]
bathroom la salle de bains [sal duh bAN]
  we want a room with bathroom nous voulons
  une chambre avec salle de bains [noo vooloN
  con shoNbr...]
  can I use your bathroom? puis-je aller aux
  toilettes? [pweeJ alay o twa-let]
battery une pile [peel]
  (for car) la batterie [batree]
be être [etr]

> Here is the present tense of the French
> verb 'to be'.
>
> **I am** je suis [Juh swee]
> **you are** *(familiar)* tu es [too eh]
> **you are** *(polite)* vous êtes [voo zet]
> **he/she/it is** il/elle est [eel/el eh]
> **we are** nous sommes [noo som]
> **you are** *(plural)* vous êtes
> **they are** ils/elles sont [eel/el soN]

  be good sois sage [swa sahJ]
  (polite) soyez sage [swy-yay...]
beach une plage [plahJ]
  on the beach à la plage [ah...]
beans des haricots [areeko]
  French beans des haricots verts [...vair]
beautiful beau/belle [bo/bel]

that was a beautiful meal ce repas était délicieux [suh ruhpa ayteh dayleess-yuh]

because parce que [parsuh-kuh]

  because of the weather à cause du temps [ah kohz...]

bed un lit [lee]

  a single bed un lit pour une personne [...poor oon pair-son]

  a double bed un lit pour deux personnes

  I'm off to bed je vais me coucher [Juh veh muh kooshay]

  you haven't changed my bed vous n'avez pas changé les draps de mon lit [voo navay pa sHoN-Jay lay dra...]

bed and breakfast la chambre et le petit déjeuner [la sHoNbr ay luh puhtee-day-Jurnay]

> ✈ If you want a UK-style B&B ask at an **Office de Tourisme** for a **chambre chez l'habitant**. If they are **agréée** that means they are registered.

bedroom une chambre [sHoNbr]

bee une abeille [a-bay]

beef du bœuf [buhf]

beer une bière [bee-yair]

  two beers, please deux bières, s'il vous plaît

> ✈ If you simply order **une bière** you may well be served more expensive bottled beer. For a draught beer ask for **un demi**.

before: before breakfast avant le petit déjeuner [a-voN...]

  before we leave avant de partir [...duh parteer]

  I haven't been here before c'est la première fois que je viens ici [seh la pruhm-yair fwa kuh Juh v-yaN ee-see]

begin: when does it begin? à quelle heure est-ce

que ça *commence*? [ah kel ur eskuh sa komONss]

beginner un débutant [day-bœtON]
   (woman) une débutante [day-bœtONt]

behind derrière [dair-yair]
   behind me derrière moi [...mwa]

Belgian belge [belJ]
   (person) un/une Belge [belJ]

Belgium la Belgique [bel-Jeek]

believe: I don't believe you je ne vous *crois* pas
   [Juh nuh voo krwa pa]
   I believe you je vous crois

bell *(in hotel, on door)* une sonnette [sonet]
   (of church) la cloche [klosh]

belong: that belongs to me c'est à moi [set ah
   mwa]
   who does this belong to? à qui est ceci? [ah
   kee eh suh-see]

below au-dessous [o duh-soo]
   below the knee au-dessous du genou [...dœ
   Juhnoo]

belt une ceinture [sAN-tœr]

bend *(in road)* un virage [vee-rahJ]

berries des baies [beh]

berth *(on ship)* une couchette [kooshet]

beside à côté de [ah ko-tay duh]

best le meilleur/la meilleure [may-yuhr]
   it's the best holiday I've ever had ce sont
   les meilleures vacances de ma vie [suh SON
   lay...vakONss duh ma vee]

better meilleur [may-yur]
   haven't you got anything better? est-ce que
   vous n'avez rien de mieux? [eskuh voo navay
   ree-yAN duh m-yuh]
   are you feeling better? est-ce que vous vous
   sentez mieux? [eskuh voo voo sONtay m-yuh]
   I'm feeling a lot better je me sens beaucoup
   mieux [Juh muh SON bo-koo...]

between entre [ONtr]

beyond plus loin que [pl∞ lwAN kuh]
  beyond the mountains au-delà des montagnes
  [o-duhla...]

bicycle une bicyclette [bee-seeklet]

bière à la pression draught beer

big grand [grON]
  a big one un grand/une grande
  that's too big c'est trop grand [seh tro...]
  have you got a bigger one? est-ce que vous
  en avez un plus grand? [eskuh voo zON navay AN
  pl∞ grON]

bike le vélo [vaylo]

bikini un bikini

bill l'addition [adeess-yON]
  could I have the bill, please? l'addition, s'il
  vous plaît [...seel voo pleh]

billets tickets

binding *(ski)* la fixation [feexass-yON]

bird un oiseau [wa-zo]

birthday l'anniversaire [anee-vair-sair]
  happy birthday! joyeux anniversaire! [Jwy-
  yuh...]
  it's my birthday c'est mon anniversaire [seh
  mON...]

biscuit un biscuit [beeskwee]

bit: just a little bit for me juste un petit peu
  pour moi [J∞st AN puhtee puh poor mwa]
  that's a bit too expensive c'est *un peu* trop
  cher [...AN puh tro shair]
  a bit of that cake un morceau de ce gâteau-là
  [AN morso...]
  a big bit un grand morceau [AN grON...]

bitter *(taste)* amer [a-mair]

black noir [nwahr]

blackout: he's had a blackout il a eu une
  syncope [eel ah ∞ ∞n sAN-kop]

blanket une couverture [koovair-toor]

bleach *(for cleaning)* de l'eau de javel [ohd JA-vel]

bleed saigner [sen-yay]

bless you! *(after sneeze)* à vos souhaits! [ah vo sweh]

blind *(cannot see)* aveugle [a-vurgl]

blister une ampoule [ONpool]

blocked *(pipe)* bouché [booshay]
   (road) bloqué [blokay]

blonde une blonde [blOND]

blood le sang [sON]
   his blood group is... son groupe sanguin est... [sON groop sON-gAN eh]
   I've got high blood pressure j'ai de la tension [jayd la tONss-yON]
   he needs a blood transfusion il faut lui faire une transfusion de sang [eel fo lwee fair con trONss-fooz-yON...]

bloody: that's bloody good! c'est vachement bien! [seh vashmON b-yAN]
   bloody hell! *(annoyed, amazed)* merde alors! [maird alor]

blouse un chemisier [shuhmeez-yay]

blue bleu [bluh]

board: full board la pension complète [pONss-yON kON-plet]
   half board la demi-pension [duhmee-]

boarding pass la carte d'embarquement [kart dONbar-kuh-mON]

boat un bateau [bato]

body le corps [kor]

boil: do we have to boil the water? est-qu'il faut faire *bouillir* l'eau? [eskeel fo fair boo-yeer lo]

boiled egg un œuf à la coque [uhf ah la kok]

bolt le verrou [vairoo]

bone un os [oss]
   (in fish) une arête [a-ret]

bonnet *(of car)* le capot [ka-po]
book un livre [leevr]
   can I book a seat for...? est-ce que je peux *réserver* une place pour...? [eskuh Juh puh rayzair-vay ɔɔn plass poor]
   I'd like to book a table for two je voudrais réserver une table pour deux [Juh voodreh rayzair-vay ɔɔn tahbl poor duh]

> *YOU MAY THEN HEAR*
> pour quelle heure? *for what time?*
> à quel nom? *and your name is?*

booking office le guichet [ghee-sheh]
bookshop une librairie [leebrairee]
boot une botte [bot]
   (of car) le coffre [kofr]
booze: I had too much booze last night j'ai trop bu hier soir [Jay tro bɔɔ yair swahr]
border la frontière [frɔNt-yair]
bored: I'm bored je m'ennuie [Juh mɔN-nwee]
boring ennuyeux [ɔN-nwee-yuh]
born: I was born in... *(year)* je suis né en... [Juh swee nay ɔN]
   go to **date**
borrow: can I borrow...? est-ce que je peux emprunter...? [eskuh Juh puh ɔNprAN-tay]
boss le patron [pa-trɔN]
   (woman) la patronne [pa-tron]
both les deux [lay duh]
   I'll take both of them je prends les deux [Juh prɔN...]
bottle une bouteille [boo-tay]
bottle-opener un ouvre-bouteille [oovruh-boo-tay]
bottom *(of person)* le derrière [dair-yair]
   at the bottom of the hill au pied de la colline [o p-yay duh la koleen]

bouchon expect delays
bouncer le videur [veedur]
bowl *(for soup etc)* un bol
box une boîte [bwat]
boy un garçon [gar-sON]
boyfriend le petit ami [puhtee ta-mee]
bra un soutien-gorge [soot-yAN-gorJ]
bracelet un bracelet [brass-leh]
brake le frein [frAN]
  could you check the brakes? est-ce que vous
  pouvez vérifier les freins? [eskuh voo poovay
  vayreef-yay lay frAN]
  I had to brake suddenly j'ai dû freiner
  brusquement [Jay doo fray-nay brooskuhmON]
  he didn't brake il n'a pas freiné [eel na pa fray-
  nay]
brandy le cognac [kon-yak]
bread du pain [pAN]
  could we have some bread and butter? est-ce
  que vous pouvez nous apporter du pain et du
  beurre? [eskuh voo poovay noo zaportay doo pAN
  ay doo bur]
  some more bread, please encore du pain, s'il
  vous plaît [ONkor...]

> ✈ The **baguette** or French stick is the stand-
> ard (best eaten the same day). Try **pain de
> campagne** or **boule**, which is crusty, good
> with cheese and keeps well.

break *(verb)* casser [ka-say]
  I think I've broken my arm je crois que je me
  suis cassé le bras [Juh krwa kuh Juh muh swee ka-
  say luh bra]
  you've broken it vous l'avez cassé [voo lavay...]
break into: my room has been broken into on
  a forcé la porte de ma chambre [ON ah forsay la
  port duh ma shONbr]

my car has been broken into ma voiture a été
forcée [ma vwatoor ah aytay forsay]
breakable fragile [fra-Jeel]
breakdown une panne [pan]
I've had a breakdown la voiture est tombée en
panne [la vwatoor ay toN-bay oN pan]
a nervous breakdown une dépresssion
nerveuse [daypress-yon nair-vurz]
breakfast le petit déjeuner [puhtee-day-Jurnay]

> ✈ In Switzerland and Belgium **déjeuner** is
> commonly used for 'breakfast'.

breast le sein [sAN]
breathe respirer [respeeray]
I can't breathe j'ai de la peine à respirer [Jay
duh la pen ah...]
bridge un pont [poN]
briefcase une serviette [sairv-yet]
**brighten up: do you think it'll brighten up
later?** pensez-vous que ça va *s'éclaircir* plus
tard? [poNsay voo kuh sa va sayklair-seer ploo tar]
brilliant *(person, idea)* brillant [bree-yoN]
(swimmer etc) accompli [akoNplee]
brilliant! génial! [Jayn-yal]
bring apporter [aportay]
could you bring it to my hotel? est-ce que
vous pouvez l'apporter à mon hôtel? [eskuh voo
poovay...]
Britain la Grande-Bretagne [groNd-bruh-tan-yuh]
British britannique [breeta-neek]
Brittany la Bretagne [bruh-tan-yuh]
**brochure: have you got any brochures
about...?** est-ce que vous avez des brochures
sur...? [eskuh voo zavay day broshoor soor]
broken cassé [ka-say]
it's broken c'est cassé [seh...]
brooch une broche [brosh]

brother: my brother mon frère [mon frair]
brown marron [maron]
  (hair) brun [brAN]
  (tanned) bronzé [bronzay]
browse: can I just browse around? est-ce que je
  peux regarder? [eskuh juh puh ruhgar-day]
bruise un bleu [bluh]
brunette une brune [broon]
brush une brosse [bross]
  (painter's) un pinceau [pAN-so]
bucket un seau [so]
buffet un buffet [boo-feh]
building un bâtiment [batee-mon]
  (residential) un immeuble [ee-murbl]
bulb une ampoule [on-pool]
  the bulb's gone l'ampoule a grillé [lon-pool ah
  gree-yay]
bumbag une banane [ba-nan]
bump: he's had a bump on the head il s'est
  tapé la tête [eel seh tapay la tet]
bumper le pare-chocs [par-shok]
bunch of flowers un bouquet de fleurs [boo-keh
  duh flur]
bunk une couchette [kooshet]
bunk beds des lits superposés [lee soopair-po-zay]
buoy une bouée [boo-ay]
bureau de change un bureau de change
bureau de tabac tobacconist, also sells stamps
and phonecards
burglar un cambrioleur [konbree-o-lur]
burgle: our flat's been burgled on a cambriolé
  notre appartement [...konbree-o-lay...]

> **they've taken all my money** ils ont pris
> tout mon argent [eel zon pree...]

burn: this meat is burnt cette viande est *brûlée*
  [...broo-lay]

my arms are burnt j'ai un coup de soleil sur les bras [Jay AN koo duh solay soor lay bra]

can you give me something for these burns? est-ce que vous avez quelque chose pour les brûlures? [eskuh voo za-vay kelkuh shohz poor lay broo-loor]

bus le bus [booss]

which bus is it for...? quel bus va à...? [kel...]

> **could you tell me when we get there?**
> est-ce que vous pouvez m'avertir quand on y arrive? [eskuh voo poovay mavair-teer KON tON nee a-reev]

✈ You usually pay the driver. You can also buy a **carnet de tickets** (book of tickets) from newsagents, tobacconists and main bus stations. Don't forget to punch your ticket on the bus. Tickets are usually valid any distance for a fixed time period (around one hour). For rides of more than two fare stages (look for the route map) you may have to punch two tickets.

business: I'm here on business je suis ici pour *affaires* [Juh swee zee-see poor afair]

none of your business! cela ne vous regarde pas! [suh-la nuh voo ruh-gard pa]

business trip un voyage d'affaires [vvy-ahJ dafair]

bus station la gare routière [Qar root-yair]

bus stop l'arrêt d'autobus [areh doto-booss]

bust la poitrine [pwa-treen]

busy (streets etc) plein de monde [plAN duh mOND] (telephone) occupé [okoopay]

are you busy? est-ce que vous êtes occupé? [eskuh voo zet...]

but mais [meh]

not...but... pas...mais... [pa...]

butcher's la boucherie [boosh-ree]
butter du beurre [bur]
button un bouton [bootON]
buy: where can I buy...? où puis-je acheter...?
  [oo pweeJ ashtay]
by: I'm here by myself je suis venu seul [Juh
  swee vuhnoo surl]
  are you by yourself? est-ce que vous êtes seul?
  [eskuh voo zet...]
  can you do it by tomorrow? est-ce que vous
  pouvez le faire pour demain? [...voo poovay luh
  fair poor duh-mAN]
  by train/car/plane en train/voiture/avion [ON...]
  I parked by the trees je me suis garé *près* des
  arbres [Juh muh swee garay preh day zahbr]
  who's it made by? c'est fabriqué *par* qui? [seh
  fabreekay par kee]

C [say]

cabbage un chou [shoo]
cabin *(on ship)* une cabine [ka-been]
cable *(electric)* un câble [kahbl]
cable car un téléphérique [taylay-fay-reek]
café un café

> ✈ Waiter service, children usually welcome;
> drinks cheaper at the bar; snacks or set
> lunch usually available; you can telephone
> from a café and there is often a special
> counter where stamps, phonecards and
> tobacco are sold (look for a red diamond
> shaped TABAC sign outside); you generally
> pay for your drinks on leaving and not
> when you order.

caisse cash desk
cake un gâteau [gato]

calculator une calculatrice [kalkoo-la-treess]

call: will you call the manager? est-ce que vous pouvez *appeler* le gérant? [eskuh voo poovay aplay luh Jay-rON]

  what is this called? comment ça s'appelle? [komON sa sa-pel]

  I'll call back later *(on phone)* je rappellerai plus tard [Juh rapeluh-ray ploo tar]

call box une cabine téléphonique [ka-been taylay-foneek]

calm calme

  calm down! calmez-vous! [kalmay-voo]

camcorder un caméscope [kamay-skop]

camera un appareil photo [apa-ray]

camp: is there somewhere we can camp? où est-ce qu'on peut *camper*? [weskON puh kONpay]

  can we camp here? est-ce qu'on peut camper ici? [...ee-see]

  we are on a camping holiday nous faisons du camping [noo fuh-zON doo kONpeeng]

campsite un terrain de camping [teh-rAN duh kONpeeng]

✈ You may be asked to leave your passport at reception.

---

can¹: a can of beer une canette de bière [kanet...]

can²: can I have...? est-ce que je *peux* avoir...? [eskuh Juh puh avwahr]

  can you...? est-ce que vous pouvez...? [eskuh voo poovay]

  (familiar) est-ce que tu peux? [eskuh too puh]

  I can't... je ne peux pas... [Juh nuh puh pa]

  I can't swim je ne sais pas nager [...nuh seh pa...]

  he/she can't... il/elle ne peut pas... [eel/el nuh puh pa]

  we can't... nous ne pouvons pas... [noo nuh poo-vON pa]

Canada le Canada [kana-da]
Canadian canadien [kanad-yAN]
  (man) un Canadien
  (woman) une Canadienne [kanad-yen]
cancel: I want to cancel my booking je veux
  annuler ma réservation [Juh vuh anꝏlay ma
  rayzair-vass-yON]
  can we cancel dinner for tonight? est-ce que
  nous pouvons décommander le dîner ce soir?
  [eskuh noo poovON day-komONday luh deenay suh
  swahr]
candle une bougie [boo-Jee]
can-opener un ouvre-boîte [oovruh-bwat]
capsize chavirer [shaveeray]
car une voiture [vwatꝏr]
  by car en voiture [ON...]
carafe une carafe [ka-raf]
caravan une caravane [kara-van]
carburettor le carburateur [karbꝏ-ra-tur]
cards les cartes [kart]
  do you play cards? est-ce que vous jouez aux
  cartes? [eskuh voo Joo-ay o...]
care: goodbye, take care au revoir et fais
  bien attention à toi [...feh b-yAN atoNss-yON ah
  twa]
careful: be careful soyez prudent [swy-yay prꝏ-
  dON]
car-ferry le ferry
car park un parking
carpet le tapis [tapee]
  (wall to wall) la moquette [moket]
carrier bag un sac
carrot une carotte [ka-rot]
carry porter [portay]
carte bleue any credit or debit card
carving une sculpture [skꝏlptꝏr]
case *(suitcase)* une valise [valeez]

cash l'argent [arJON]
  I haven't any cash je n'ai pas de monnaie
  (change) [Juh nuh pa duh moneh]
  I'll pay cash je paye comptant [Juh peh KON-tON]
  will you cash this cheque for me? est-ce que
  vous pouvez me donner de l'argent contre ce
  chèque? [eskuh voo poovay muh donay...]
cash desk la caisse [kess]
casino un casino [kazee-no]
casse-croûte snack
cassette une cassette [ka-set]
cassette player un lecteur de cassettes [lektur
  duh ka-set]
castle un château [shato]

✈ Most close on Tuesdays.

cat un chat [sha]
catch: where do we catch the bus? où est-ce
  qu'on *prend* le bus? [weskON prON luh booss]
  he's caught a bug il a attrapé un virus [eel ah
  atrapay AN veerooss]
cathedral la cathédrale [katay-dral]
catholic catholique [katoleek]
cave une grotte [grot]
CD un CD [say-day]
CD-player une platine CD [plateen say-day]
cédez le passage give way
ceiling le plafond [pla-fON]
cellophane le cellophane [selofahn]
cent un centime [sONteem]
centigrade centigrade [sONtee-grad]

✈ C/5 x 9 + 32 = F

centigrade	-5	0	10	15	21	30	36.9
Fahrenheit	23	32	50	59	70	86	98.4

centimetre un centimètre [sONtee-metr]

✈ 1 cm = 0.39 inches

central central [soN-tral]
  with central heating avec le chauffage central
  [...sho-fahJ...]
centre le centre [soNtr]
  how do we get to the centre? comment est-
  ce qu'on va dans le centre? [komoN eskoN va
  doN luh...]
centre-ville city centre, town centre
certain *(sure)* certain/certaine [sair-tAN/sair-ten]
  are you certain? est-ce que vous en êtes sûr?
  [eskuh voo zoN net soor]
certificate un certificat [sairtee-fee-ka]
chain une chaîne [shen]
chair une chaise [shez]
  (armchair) un fauteuil [fo-tuh-ee]
chairlift le télésiège [taylays-yeJ]
chambermaid la femme de chambre [fam duh
  shoNbr]
chambres rooms to let
champagne du champagne [shoN-pan-yuh]
change *(verb)* changer [shoNJay]
  could you change this into euros? est-ce que
  vous pouvez me changer ça en euros? [eskuh
  voo poovay muh shoNJay sa oN urro]
  I haven't any change je n'ai pas de monnaie
  [Juh nay pa duh moneh]
  do you have change for 100 euros? est-ce
  que vous avez la monnaie de cent euros? [eskuh
  voo zavay la moneh duh...]
  do we have to change trains? est-ce qu'il faut
  changer? [eskeel fo...]
channel: the Channel la Manche [moNsh]
Channel Islands les îles anglo-normandes [eel
  oN-glo nor-moNd]
Channel Tunnel le tunnel sous la Manche [toonel

soo la mONsh]

chantier roadworks

charge: what will you charge? combien est-ce
que ça va coûter? [kONb-yAN eskuh sa va kootay]
who's in charge? qui est le responsable? [kee
eh luh respONsahbl]

chart *(map)* une carte maritime [kart maree-
teem]

chaud hot

chaussée glissante slippery road surface

cheap bon marché [bON marshay]
have you got something cheaper? est-ce que
vous avez quelque chose de moins cher? [eskuh
voo zavay kelkuh shohz duh mwAN shair]

cheat: I've been cheated je me suis fait avoir
[Juh muh swee feh avwahr]

check: will you check? est-ce que vous pouvez
vérifier? [eskuh voo poovay vayreef-yay]
I've checked j'ai vérifié [Jay vayreef-yay]
we checked in *(at hotel)* nous sommes arrivés
[noo som zareevay]
we checked out *(from hotel)* nous sommes
partis [...partee]

check-in desk le comptoir d'enregistrement
[kONtwahr dON-reJeestruh-mON]

check-in time l'heure d'enregistrement [ur dON-
reJeestruh-mON]

cheek *(of face)* la joue [Joo]

cheeky effronté [efrONtay]

cheerio au revoir [o ruh-vwahr]

cheers *(toast)* santé [sON-tay]
(thanks) merci [mairsee]

cheese du fromage [fromahJ]

➤ A huge range. Milder cheeses include **le
brie, le cantal, le comté, l'emmental, le
morbier, le Port-Salut, le Saint-Paulin;**

stronger varieties: **le bleu (d'Auvergne), le camembert, le munster, le reblochon, le roquefort, le Saint-Nectaire.**

cheeseburger un 'cheeseburger'
chef le chef
chemist's une pharmacie [farma-see]

> ✈ Look for the green cross sign. The address of a 24-hour or Sunday-duty **pharmacie de garde** will be on the door of every chemist.

cheque un chèque [shek]
cheque book le carnet de chèques [karneh duh shek]
cheque card la carte d'identité bancaire [kart deedON-tee-tay bON-kair]

> ✈ Doesn't exist in France. Use your passport instead.

chest la poitrine [pwa-treen]
chewing gum du chewing-gum [shween-gom]
chicken *(to eat)* du poulet [pooleh]
chickenpox la varicelle [varee-sel]
child un/une enfant [ON-fON]
child minder une nourrice [nooreess]
children les enfants [ON-fON]
  a children's portion une portion pour enfants [pors-yON poor...]

> ✈ Children are usually welcome in restaurants and cafés.

chin le menton [mON-tON]
china la porcelaine [por-suh-len]
chips des frites [freet]
  (in casino) des jetons [juhtON]
chocolate du chocolat [shokola]
  a hot chocolate un chocolat chaud [...sho]

a box of chocolates une boîte de chocolats [bwat...]

chop: pork/lamb chop une côtelette de porc/d'agneau [kot-let duh por/dan-yo]

Christian name le prénom [pray-nON]

Christmas Noël [no-el]

  on Christmas Eve la veille de Noël [vay...]

  Happy Christmas Joyeux Noël [Jwy-yuh...]

> ✈ Christmas Eve is usually the occasion for a big meal (**le réveillon de Noël**) with family or friends.

church une église [ay-gleez]

chutes de pierres falling rocks

cider du cidre [seedr]

cigar un cigare [see-gar]

cigarette une cigarette [seega-ret]

cinema un cinéma [seenay-ma]

circle un cercle [sairkl]

  (in cinema) le balcon [bal-kON]

circulation alternée contraflow

city une ville [veel]

city centre le centre-ville [sONtruh-veel]

claim *(insurance)* une déclaration de sinistre [dayklarass-yON duh seeneestruh]

claret du Bordeaux rouge [bordo rooJ]

clarify clarifier [klareef-yay]

clean *(adjective)* propre [propr]

  it's not clean ce n'est pas propre [suh neh pa...]

  my room hasn't been cleaned today on n'a pas nettoyé ma chambre aujourd'hui [ON na pa netwy-yay ma shONbr oJoordwee]

cleansing cream la crème démaquillante [krem dayma-kee-yONt]

clear: I'm not clear about it je n'ai pas bien compris [Juh nay pa b-yAN kONpree]

clever intelligent [ANtay-lee-JON]

(skilful) habile [abeel]

climate le climat [klee-ma]

climb: we're going to climb... nous allons escalader... [noo zalON eska-la-day]

climber un/une alpiniste [alpee-neest]

climbing boots des chaussures d'escalade [sho-soor deska-lad]

clip *(for ski)* l'attache [atash]

cloakroom *(for clothes)* le vestiaire [vest-yair]

clock une horloge [orloJ]

close¹ près [preh]

(weather) lourd [loor]

is it close to...? est-ce que c'est près de...? [eskuh seh...]

close²: when do you close? quand est-ce que vous *fermez*? [kONteskuh voo fairmay]

closed fermé [fairmay]

cloth le tissu [tee-soo]

(rag) un chiffon [shee-fON]

clothes les vêtements [vet-mON]

clothes peg une pince à linge [pANss ah lANJ]

cloud un nuage [noo-ahJ]

clubbing: we're going clubbing nous allons en boîte [noo zalON ON bwat]

clutch l'embrayage [ONbreh-yahJ]

the clutch is slipping l'embrayage patine [...pa-teen]

coach le car

coach party un car de touristes

coach trip une excursion en car [exkoors-yON ON...]

coast la côte [koht]

at the coast sur la côte [soor...]

coastguard le garde-côte [gard-koht]

coat un manteau [mONto]

cockroach un cafard [ka-far]

coffee un café [ka-fay]

a white coffee un café au lait [...o leh]

> ✈ If you order **un café**, you'll get a small
> espresso (also called **un petit café**). If you
> want it with milk ask for **un café crème**
> [...krem] or, for a bigger one, **un grand
> crème**.

coin une pièce de monnaie [pee-yess duh moneh]
coke® un coca-cola
cold froid [frwa]
  I'm cold j'ai froid [Jay...]
  I've got a cold j'ai un rhume [Jay AN room]
collapse: he's collapsed il s'est effondré [eel seh
  ayfON-dray]
collar le col

✈ UK:	14	14.5	15	15.5	16	16.5	17
France:	36	37	38	39	41	42	43

collect: I've come to collect... je viens chercher...
  [Juh v-yAN shair-shay]
colour la couleur [koolur]
  have you any other colours? est-ce que vous
  avez d'autres couleurs? [eskuh voo zavay dohtr...]
comb un peigne [pen-yuh]
come venir [vuh-neer]
  I come from London je viens de Londres [Juh
  v-yAN...]
  when is he coming? quand est-ce qu'il arrive?
  [kONtesk-eel areev]
  we came here yesterday nous sommes arrivés
  ici hier [noo som zaree-vay...]
  come here venez ici [vuh-nay zee-see]
  come with me venez avec moi [vuh-nay...]
  come on! allons! [alON]
  oh, come on! *(disbelief)* vous plaisantez! [voo
  plezONtay]
comfortable confortable [kONfor-tahbl]
company *(business)* la société [soss-yay-tay]

you're good company j'aime votre compagnie
[Jem votr kONpan-yee]

compartment *(in train)* un compartiment
[kONpartee-mON]

compass une boussole [boo-sol]

compensation une indemnisation [ANdemnee-
zass-yON]

I want compensation je veux être dédommagé
[Juh vuh zetr daydoma-Jay]

complain se plaindre [suh plANdr]

I want to complain about my room je veux
faire une *réclamation* au sujet de ma chambre
[Juh vuh fair œn rayklamass-yON o sœ-Jeh duh...]

complet full, no vacancies

completely complètement [kONplet-mON]

complicated: it's very complicated c'est très
compliqué [seh treh kONplee-kay]

compliment: my compliments to the chef mes
compliments au chef [kONplee-mON o...]

composter: prière de composter votre billet
please punch your ticket here

compulsory: is it compulsory? est-ce que c'est
obligatoire? [eskuh seh tobleega-twahr]

computer un ordinateur [ordeen-atur]

concert un concert [kONsair]

concierge caretaker

concussion une commotion cérébrale [komohss-
yON sayray-bral]

condition la condition [kONdeess-yON]

it's not in very good condition ce n'est pas en
très bon état [suh nay pa zON treh bON nay-ta]

condom un préservatif [prayzairvateef]

conference une conférence [kONfay-rONss]

confirm confirmer [kONfeermay]

confuse: you're confusing me vous
m'embrouillez [voo mON-brœ-yay]

congés holiday

congratulations! félicitations! [faylee-see-tass-yON]

conjunctivitis une conjonctivite [kONJONk-tee-veet]

conman l'arnaqueur [arnakur]

connection *(travel)* la correspondance [korespON-dONss]

connoisseur un connaisseur [konessur]

conscious conscient [kONss-yON]

consciousness: he's lost consciousness il a perdu connaissance [eel ah pairdoo koneh-sONss]

consigne left luggage

constipation la constipation [kONstee-pa-syON]

consul le consul [kON-sool]

consulate le consulat [kON-soola]

contact: how can I contact...? comment est-ce que je peux contacter...? [komON eskuh Juh puh kONtaktay]

contact lenses les lentilles de contact [lONtee...]

convenient pratique [prateek]

cook: it's not cooked ce n'est pas cuit [suh nay pa kwee]

you're a good cook vous faites bien la cuisine [voo fet b-yAN la kwee-zeen]

cooker la cuisinière [kweezeen-yair]

cool frais/fraîche [freh/fresh]

(great) super [soopair]

corkscrew un tire-bouchon [teer-booshON]

corner un coin [kwAN]

(bend) un virage [vee-rahJ]

can we have a corner table? est-ce qu'on peut avoir une table dans un coin? [eskON puh avwahr oon tahbl dON zAN kwAN]

on the corner au coin de la rue [o kwAN duh la roo]

in the corner dans le coin [dON...]

cornflakes des 'cornflakes'

correct correct

correspondances other lines

Corsica la Corse [korss]

cosmetics des produits de beauté [prodwee duh bo-tay]

cost: what does it cost? combien ça coûte? [koNb-yAN sa koot]

> **that's too much** c'est trop [seh tro]
> **I'll take it** je le prends [Juh luh proN]

cot un lit d'enfant [lee doN-foN]

cotton du coton [kotoN]

cotton wool du coton hydrophile [kotoN eedro-feel]

couchette une couchette [kooshet]

cough la toux [too]

cough sweets des pastilles pour la toux [pastee poor la too]

could: could you please...? est-ce que vous pouvez...? [eskuh voo poovay]

could I have...? est-ce que je peux avoir...? [eskuh Juh puh avwahr]

we couldn't... nous n'avons pas pu... [noo na-voN pa poo]

country le pays [payee]

in the country(side) à la campagne [ah la koN-pan-yuh]

couple: a couple of... (two) deux ou trois... [duh oo trwa]

(a few) quelques... [kelkuh]

courier le/la guide [gheed]

course: of course bien sûr [b-yAN soor]

court: I'll take you to court je vais vous poursuivre en justice [Juh veh voo poorsweevr oN Joosteess]

cousin: my cousin (male) mon cousin [koozAN]

(female) ma cousine [koozeen]

cover: keep him covered couvrez-le bien

[koovray-luh b-yAN]

cover charge le couvert [koovair]

cow une vache [vash]

crab un crabe [krab]

craftshop une boutique d'artisanat [...artee-za-na]

crap: this is crap c'est nul [seh nool]

crash: there's been a crash il y a eu une collision
  [eelya oo oon koleez-yON]

crash helmet un casque [kask]

crazy fou/folle [foo/fol]
  you're crazy vous êtes fou/folle [voo zet...]
  that's crazy c'est de la folie [seh duh la folee]

cream de la crème [krem]

credit card une carte de crédit [kart duh kray-dee]

crêperie pancake shop/stall

crisps des chips [sheeps]

cross *(verb)* traverser [travair-say]

crossroads le carrefour [kar-foor]

crowded bondé [bONday]
  it's crowded il y a beaucoup de monde [eelya
  bo-koo duh mOND]

cruise une croisière [krwaz-yair]

crutch *(for invalid)* une béquille [bay-kee]

cry: don't cry ne pleurez pas [nuh plur-ray pa]

cup une tasse [tass]
  a cup of coffee un café [ka-fay]

cupboard une armoire [arm-wahr]

curry le curry [kuh-ree]

curtains les rideaux [reedo]

cushion un coussin [koo-sAN]

Customs la douane [dwahn]

cut *(verb)* couper [koopay]
  I've cut myself je me suis coupé [Juh muh swee
  koopay]

cycle: can we cycle there? est-ce qu'on peut y
  aller à vélo? [eskON puh ee alay ah vaylo]

cyclist un/une cycliste [seekleest]

cylinder-head gasket le joint de culasse [JWAN duh koolass]

D [day]

dad: my dad mon père [MON pair]

damage: I'll pay for the damage je rembourserai les *dégâts* [Juh RONboor-suh-ray lay day-ga]

damaged abîmé [abeemay]

damn! zut! [zoot]

damp humide [oomeed]

dames ladies

dance: would you like to dance? voulez-vous danser? [voolay-voo dON-say]

dangerous dangereux [doNJ-ruh]

dark foncé [foN-say]

   when does it get dark? quand est-ce que la nuit tombe? [kONteskuh la nwee tONb]

   dark blue bleu foncé [bluh...]

darling chéri/chérie [shay-ree]

date: what's the date? quelle est la date d'aujourd'hui? [kel eh la dat doJoordwee]

   can we make a date? *(romantic)* est-ce que nous pouvons nous revoir? [eskuh noo poovON noo ruh-vwahr]

---

   in 1983 en mille neuf cent quatre-vingt-trois [meel nurf soN ka-truh-vAN-trwa]

   in 2004 en deux mille quatre

Use the ordinary numbers for dates (go to page 159).

   it's the second of February c'est le deux février

The exception is for the first.

> **it's the first of February** c'est le premier
> février [pruhm-yay...]

dates *(fruit)* des dattes [dat]
daughter: my daughter ma fille [...fee]
day un jour [Joor]
  the day after le lendemain [lONduh-mAN]
  the day before la veille [vay]
dazzle: his lights were dazzling me ses phares
  m'éblouissaient [say far maybloo-ee-say]
dead mort [mor]
deaf sourd [soor]
deal: it's a deal d'accord! [da-kor]
  will you deal with it? est-ce que vous pouvez
  vous en charger? [eskuh voo poovay voo zON
  shar-Jay]
dear *(expensive)* cher [shair]
  Dear Christophe cher Christophe
  Dear Raphaëlle chère Raphaëlle
  Dear Mr/Mrs Mongeard cher Monsieur/
  Madame
December décembre [day-sONbr]
deck le pont [pON]
deckchair une chaise longue [shez lONg]
declare: I have nothing to declare je n'ai rien à
  déclarer [Juh nay ree-yAN ah daykla-ray]
deep profond [profON]
défense d'entrer no entry
de-icer le dégivreur [day-Jee-vrur]
delay: the flight was delayed le vol a eu du
  retard [luh vol ah oo doo ruh-tar]
deliberately exprès [ex-preh]
delicate délicat [daylee-ka]
delicious délicieux [dayleess-yuh]
de luxe de luxe [duh looks]
dent une bosse [boss]
dentist un/une dentiste [dON-teest]

> *YOU MAY HEAR*
> quelle dent vous fait mal? *which tooth is hurting?*
> ouvrez grand la bouche *open wide*
> rincez *rinse out*

dentures le dentier [doNt-yay]
deny: I deny it ce n'est pas vrai [suh nuh pa vreh]
deodorant un déodorant [day-o-doroN]
dépannage breakdown recovery service
departure le départ [day-par]
departure lounge la salle d'embarquement [sal doNbar-kuh-moN]
depend: it depends ça dépend [day-poN]
   it depends on... ça dépend de...
deposit *(downpayment)* un acompte [a-koNt]
   (security) une caution [kohss-yoN]
depressed déprimé [daypreemay]
depth la profondeur [profoN-dur]
desperate: I'm desperate for a drink je meurs de soif [Juh mur duh swaf]
dessert un dessert [day-sair]

> ✈ Typical desserts include: **une tarte Tatin** (apple pie), **une crème brûlée** (crème caramel), **une glace à la vanille** (vanilla ice cream).

destination la destination [desteenass-yoN]
detergent un détergent [daytair-JON]
detour un détour [day-toor]
develop: could you develop these? est-ce que vous pouvez me développer ces pellicules? [eskuh voo poovay muh dayv-lopay say peleekool]
diabetic diabétique [dee-a-bay-teek]
diamond un diamant [dee-a-moN]
diarrhoea la diarrhée [dee-a-ray]
   have you got something for diarrhoea?

est-ce que vous avez quelque chose contre la
diarrhée? [eskuh voo zavay kelkuh shohz kONtr...]
diary un agenda [aJON-da]
dictionary un dictionnaire [deeks-yonair]
didn't *go to* **not**
die mourir [moo-reer]
diesel du gas-oil [gaz-wal]
diet un régime [ray-Jeem]
  I'm on a diet je suis au régime [Juh swee zo...]
different différent [deefay-rON]
  can I have a different room? est-ce que je
  peux avoir une autre chambre? [eskuh Juh puh
  avvwahr oon ohtr shONbr]
difficult difficile [deefee-seel]
dinghy *(sailing)* un dériveur [dayree-vur]
  (rubber) un canot pneumatique [ka-no pnuh-
  mateek]
dining room la salle à manger [sala-mONJay]
dinner *(evening)* le dîner [deenay]

> ✈ In Switzerland and Belgium **souper** [soopay]
> is commonly used for 'dinner'.

dinner jacket un smoking
direct *(adjective)* direct [dee-rekt]
  does it go direct? est-ce que c'est direct?
  [eskuh seh...]
dirty sale [sal]
disabled handicapé [ONdee-ka-pay]
disappear disparaître [deespa-retr]
  it's just disappeared ça a disparu [sa ah
  deesparoo]
disappointing décevant [dayss-vON]
disco une discothèque [-tek]
discount un rabais [ra-beh]
disgusting dégoûtant [daygoo-tON]
dish un plat [pla]
dishonest malhonnête [mal-onet]

disinfectant un désinfectant [dayzAN-fek-tON]

disposable camera un appareil jetable [aparay juh-tahbl]

distance la distance [deestONss]
  in the distance au loin [o lwAN]

distress signal un signal de détresse [seen-yal duh day-tress]

disturb: the noise is disturbing us le bruit nous *dérange* [brwee noo day-rONJ]

diving board le plongeoir [plON-Jwahr]

divorced divorcé [deevor-say]

do faire [fair]
  what are you doing tonight? qu'est-ce que vous faites ce soir? [keskuh voo fet suh swahr] *(familiar)* qu'est-ce que tu fais ce soir? [...too feh...]
  how do you do it? comment ça se fait? [komON sa suh feh]
  will you do it for me? est-ce que vous pouvez le faire pour moi? [eskuh voo poovay luh fair poor mwa]
  I've never done it before je n'ai jamais fait ça [Juh nay Ja-meh feh sa]
  he did it! *(it was him)* c'est lui qui l'a fait! [seh lwee kee...]
  I was doing 60 (kph) je roulais à soixante [Juh roo-lay ah swa-sONt]
  how do you do? comment allez-vous? [komONt alay-voo]

doctor un médecin [mayd-sAN]
  I need a doctor j'ai besoin de voir un médecin [Jay buh-zwAN duh vwahr...]

✈ There is a reciprocal health agreement between UK and France. Pick up a form E111 from your local post office in the UK. This will entitle you to a partial refund on some medical services, which you must claim while still in France. You will still have to pay the French GP first, and keep the **feuille de soins** to get your refund.

YOU MAY HEAR
est-ce que vous avez déjà eu ça? *have you had this before?*
où est-ce que ça vous fait mal? *where does it hurt?*
est-ce vous prenez des médicaments? *are you taking any medication?*
prenez-en deux/trois *take two/three of these*
deux/trois fois par jour *twice/three times a day*
aux heures des repas *at mealtimes*

---

document un document [dokœ-moN]
dog un chien [shee-AN]
don't! stop!
 go to **not**
door la porte [port]
dosage la dose [dohz]
douane customs
double room une chambre pour deux [shoNbr poor duh]
 (with double bed) une chambre avec grand lit [...groN lee]
double whisky un double whisky [doobl...]
douche shower
Dover Douvres [doovr]
down: down there là-bas [la-ba]
 get down! descendez! [day-soN-day]
 it's just down the road c'est à quelques pas d'ici [set ah kelkuh pa dee-see]
downstairs en bas [oN ba]
drain un égout [ay-goo]

(in bathroom) le tuyau d'écoulement [twee-yo
daykool-mON]
drawing pin une punaise [pœnez]
dress une robe [rob]

| ✈ UK: | 8 | 10 | 12 | 14 | 16 | 18 | 20 |
| France: | 36 | 38 | 40 | 42 | 44 | 46 | 48 |

dressing *(for cut)* le pansement [pONss-mON]
(for salad) l'assaisonnement [asezon-mON]
drink *(verb)* boire [bwahr]
(noun) une boisson [bwa-sON]
  something to drink quelque chose à boire
  [kelkuh shohz ah...]
  would you like a drink? désirez-vous boire
  quelque chose? [dayzee-ray voo...]
  I don't drink je ne bois pas d'alcool [Juh nuh
  bwa pa dal-kol]
drinkable: is the water drinkable? est-ce que
l'eau est *potable*? [eskuh lo eh potahbl]
drive conduire [kON-dweer]
  I've been driving all day j'ai *roulé* toute la
  journée [Jay roo-lay...]

> ✈ Watch out for **priorité** rules. In general cars
> coming from the right have priority unless
> you are on a **voie prioritaire**. Children
> under 10 must sit in the rear seats.

driver le conducteur [kONdook-tur]
  (woman) la conductrice [kONdook-treess]
driving licence le permis de conduire [pairmee
duh kON-dweer]
droguerie drugstore, sells household goods,
aspirin, toiletries etc
drown: he's drowning il se noie [eel suh nwa]
drug un médicament [maydee-ka-mON]
  (narcotic etc) la drogue [drog]
drug dealer un dealer

(woman) une dealeuse [deelurz]

drunk *(adjective)* ivre [eevr]

dry *(adjective)* sec/sèche [sek/sesh]

dry-clean nettoyer à sec [netwy-yay ah sek]

dry-cleaner's un pressing

due: when's the bus due? quand est-ce que le bus
doit arriver? [kONT eskuh luh bœss dwa taree-vay]

during pendant [pON-dON]

dust la poussière [poos-yair]

duty-free shop la boutique hors taxe [...or tax]

DVD un DVD [day-vay-day]

E [ay]

each: can we have one each? est-ce que nous
pouvons en avoir un/une *chacun/chacune?*
[eskuh noo poovON ON navwahr AN/œn shakAN/
shakœn]

  how much are they each? combien coûte
l'unité? [kONb-yAN koot lœneetay]

ear l'oreille [oray]

  I've got earache j'ai mal à l'oreille [Jay...]

early tôt [toh]

  (ahead of time) en avance [ON avONss]

  we want to leave a day earlier nous voulons
partir un jour plus tôt [noo voolON parteer AN
Joor plœ toh]

earring une boucle d'oreille [bookl doray]

east l'est [est]

Easter Pâques [pahk]

Easter Monday le lundi de Pâques [lAN-dee duh
pahk]

easy facile [fa-seel]

eat manger [mONJay]

  something to eat quelque chose à manger
[kelkuh shohz...]

eau potable drinking water

egg un œuf [urf]
either: either...or... ou...ou... [oo...]
 I don't like either aucun/aucune des deux ne me plaît [o-kAN/o-kœn day duh...]
elastic élastique [aylasteek]
elastic band un élastique [aylasteek]
elbow le coude [kood]
electric électrique [aylek-treek]
electric fire un radiateur électrique [rad-yatur aylek-treek]
electrician un électricien [aylek-treess-yAN]
electricity l'électricité [aylek-tree-see-tay]

✈ You'll need a plug adaptor. French plugs have two round pins. Voltage is 220 as in the UK.

électroménager electrical appliances
elegant élégant [aylay-gON]
else: something else quelque chose d'autre [kelkuh shohz dohtr]
 somewhere else ailleurs [I-yur]
 let's go somewhere else allons ailleurs [alON...]
 who else? qui d'autre? [kee dohtr]
 or else sinon [see-nON]
email un 'e-mail'
 why don't you email me? pourquoi ne m'envoyez-vous pas un e-mail? [poor-kwa nuh mONvwy-yay-voo pa AN...]
email address l'adresse 'e-mail' [ad-ress...]
 what's your email address? quelle est votre adresse e-mail? [kel eh votr...]

> *YOU MAY THEN HEAR*
> **mon adresse e-mail est...**
> arobase...point...
> *my email address is...*
> *at...dot...*

embarrassed gêné [Jay-nay]

embarrassing embarrassant [ONbara-sON]
embassy l'ambassade [ONbasad]
emergency une urgence [œr-JONss]

➤ Emergency numbers will be given on all
phone dials. You can also dial 112 on a
mobile for any emergency service.

empty vide [veed]
end la fin [fAN]
  when does it end? quand est-ce que ça finit?
  [kON teskuh sa fee-nee]
engaged *(telephone, toilet)* occupé [okœpay]
  (person) fiancé [fee-ON-say]
engagement ring la bague de fiançailles [bag
  duh fee-ONsI]
engine le moteur [mo-tur]
engine trouble des ennuis mécaniques [ON-nwee
  maykaneek]
England l'Angleterre [ONgluh-tair]
English anglais [ON-gleh]
  the English les Anglais
Englishman un Anglais [ON-gleh]
Englishwoman une Anglaise [ON-glez]
enjoy: I enjoyed it very much j'ai beaucoup
  aimé [Jay bo-koo ay-may]
enlargement *(photo)* un agrandissement [agRON-
  deess-mON]
enormous énorme [ay-norm]
enough assez [assay]
  that's not big enough ce n'est pas assez grand
  [suh neh pa...gRON]
  I don't have enough money je n'ai pas assez
  d'argent [Juh nay pa...]
  thank you, that's enough merci, ça suffit [...sa
  sœ-fee]
ensuite: is it ensuite? est-ce qu'il y a une salle de
  bains dans la chambre? [eskeelya œn sal duh bAN

dON la shONbr]

entertainment les animations [aneemass-yON]

entrance l'entrée [ON-tray]

envelope une enveloppe [ONv-lop]

error une erreur [air-rur]

escalator un escalier roulant [eskal-yay rooLON]

especially spécialement [spayss-yal-mON]

essential essentiel [aysONss-yel]

e-ticket un billet électronique [bee-yeh aylektroneek]

euro un euro [urro]

Europe l'Europe [ur-rop]

even: even the British même les Britanniques [mem...]

evening le soir [swahr]

  in the evening le soir

  this evening ce soir [suh...]

  good evening bonsoir (monsieur/madame/ mademoiselle) [bON-swahr...]

evening dress (for man) la tenue de soirée [tuh-noo duh swah-ray]

  (for woman) la robe de soirée [rob...]

ever: have you ever been to...? est-ce que vous êtes déjà allé à...? [eskuh voo zet day-Ja alay ah]

every chaque [shak]

  every day chaque jour [shak Joor]

everyone tout le monde [too luh mONd]

everything tout [too]

everywhere partout [partoo]

exact exact [eg-zakt]

example un exemple [eg-zONpl]

  for example par exemple

excellent excellent [eksay-lON]

except: except me à part moi [ah par...]

excess baggage l'excédent de bagages [eksay-dON duh bagahJ]

exchange rate le taux de change [toh duh shONJ]

excursion une excursion [exkoorss-yON]
excuse me pardon [pardON]

> ✈ To get someone's attention you can also say
> **monsieur** [muh-syuh] to a man, **madame**
> [ma-dam] to a woman or **mademoiselle**
> [mad-mwa-zel] to a younger woman.

exhaust *(on car)* le pot d'échappement [po
dayshap-mON]
exhausted épuisé [aypwee-zay]
exhibition une exposition [expo-zeess-yON]
exit la sortie [sortee]
expect: she's expecting elle attend un bébé
[el atON AN bay-bay]
expenses: it's on expenses ça va sur la note de
frais [sa va soor la not duh freh]
expensive cher [shair]
expert un/une spécialiste [spayss-yaleest]
explain expliquer [explee-kay]
　would you explain that slowly? pouvez-vous
　expliquer cela lentement? [poovay-voo...suhla
　lONtuh-mON]
extension cable une rallonge [ralONJ]
extra: an extra day un jour de plus [...duh ploos]
　is that extra? est-ce que c'est en supplément?
　[eskuh seh tON sooplay-mON]
extremely extrêmement [extremuhmON]
eye l'œil [uh-ee]
　eyes les yeux [yuh]
eyebrow le sourcil [soorseel]
eyebrow pencil un crayon à sourcils [kreh-yON ah
soor-seel]
eyeliner un 'eye-liner'
eye shadow le fard à paupières [far ah pohp-yair]
eye witness un témoin oculaire [tay-mwAN okoo-
lair]

F [ef]

face le visage [vee-zahJ]
face mask *(for diving)* un masque de plongée
[...duh plonJay]
fact le fait [feh]
factory une usine [œzeen]
Fahrenheit 'Fahrenheit'

✈ F - 32 x 5/9 = C							
Fahrenheit	23	32	50	59	70	86	98.4
centigrade	-5	0	10	15	21	30	36.9

faint: she's fainted elle s'est évanouie [el set
ayvan-wee]
fair *(fun-, trade)* une foire [fwahr]
  that's not fair ce n'est pas juste [suh neh pa
  Jœst]
fake un faux/une fausse [fo/fohss]
fall: he's fallen il est tombé [eel eh toNbay]
false faux/fausse [fo/fohs]
false teeth un dentier [doNt-yay]
family la famille [fa-mee]
fan *(cooling)* le ventilateur [voNtee-latur]
  (supporter) un supporter [sœpor-tair]
fan belt la courroie du ventilateur [koo-rwa dœ
voNtee-latur]
far loin [lwaN]
  is it far? es-ce que c'est loin? [eskuh seh lwaN]
  how far is it? c'est à quelle distance d'ici? [seh
  ta kel deestoNss dee-see]
fare *(travel)* le prix du billet [pree dœ bee-yeh]
farm une ferme [fairm]
farther plus loin [plœ lwaN]
fashion la mode [mod]
fast *(adjective)* rapide [ra-peed]
  don't speak so fast ne parlez pas si vite [nuh

parlay pa see veet]

fat *(adjective)* gros [gro]

father: my father mon père [mON pair]

fathom une brasse [brass]

fault *(defect)* un défaut [day-fo]
  it's not my fault ce n'est pas de ma faute [suh nuh pahd ma foht]

faulty défectueux [dayfek-too-uh]

favourite *(adjective)* préféré [prayfay-ray]

fax un fax
  can you fax this for me? est-ce que vous pouvez faxer ça pour moi? [eskuh voo poovay faxay sa poor mwa]

February février [fayvree-yay]

fed-up: I'm fed-up j'en ai assez [JON nay assay]

feel: I feel like... *(I want)* j'ai envie de... [Jay ON-vee duh]

felt-tip un feutre [furtr]

femmes women

fermé closed

ferry le ferry [fairee]

fetch: will you come and fetch me? est-ce que vous pouvez venir me *chercher*? [eskuh voo poovay vuh-neer muh shair-shay]

fever la fièvre [fee-yevr]

few: only a few quelques-uns/quelques-unes seulement [kelkuh-zAN/kelkuh-zOON surlmON]
  a few days quelques jours [kelkuh JOOr]

fiancé le fiancé [fee-yON-say]

fiancée la fiancée [fee-yON-say]

fiddle: it's a fiddle c'est malhonnête [seh malonet]

field un champ [shON]

fifty-fifty moitié-moitié [mwat-yay-mwat-yay]

figs des figues [feeg]

figure *(number)* un chiffre [sheefr]
  (of person) la ligne [leen-yuh]

fill: fill her up faites le plein [fet luh plAN]

to fill in a form remplir un formulaire [rON-pleer AN formoo-lair]

fillet un filet [feeleh]

filling *(in tooth)* un plombage [plON-bahJ]

film un film

(for camera) une pellicule [peleekool]

do you have this type of film? avez-vous ce genre de pellicule? [avay-voo suh JONr duh...]

filter un filtre [feeltr]

find trouver [troovay]

if you find it si vous le/la trouvez [see voo luh/la troovay]

I've found a... j'ai trouvé un/une... [Jay...]

fine *(weather)* beau [bo]

ok, that's fine d'accord ça va [da-kor sa va]

a 200 euro fine une amende de deux cents euros [oon ah-mONd duh...]

finger le doigt [dwa]

fingernail l'ongle [ONgl]

finish: I haven't finished je n'ai pas fini [Juh nay pa fee-nee]

when does it finish? quand est-ce que ça finit? [kON teskuh sa fee-nee]

fire un feu [fuh]

(house on fire etc) un incendie [ANsoN-dee]

fire! au feu! [o fuh]

can we light a fire here? est-ce qu'on peut faire du feu ici? [eskON puh fair doo fuh ee-see]

it's not firing *(car)* il y a un défaut à l'allumage [eelya AN day-fo ah laloo-mahJ]

fire brigade les pompiers [pONp-yay]

✈ Dial 18. On your mobile dial 112.

fire extinguisher un extincteur [ex-tANk-tur]

first premier [pruhm-yay]

I was first j'étais le premier/la première [...pruhm-yair]

first aid les premiers secours [pruhm-yay suh-koor]

first aid kit la trousse de secours [trooss duh suh-koor]

first class *(travel)* première classe [pruhm-yair klass]

first name le prénom [pray-nON]

fish le poisson [pwa-sON]

fishing la pêche [pesh]

fit *(healthy)* en bonne condition physique [ON bon kONdeess-yON fee-zeek]
(for sport) en forme [ON form]
it doesn't fit me ce n'est pas la bonne taille [suh neh pa la bon tI]

fix: can you fix it? *(repair)* est-ce que vous pouvez le/la *réparer*? [eskuh voo poovay luh/la raypa-ray]

fizzy gazeux [ga-zuh]

flag le drapeau [dra-po]
(ship's) le pavillon [pavee-yON]

flash *(photography)* un flash

flat *(adjective)* plat [pla]
(apartment) un appartement [apartuh-mON]
I've got a flat (tyre) j'ai un pneu à plat [Jay AN pnuh...]

flavour la parfum [par-fAN]

flea une puce [pœss]

flies *(on trousers)* la braguette [bra-get]

flight un vol

flight number le numéro de vol [noomay-ro duh...]

flippers des palmes [palm]

flirt *(verb)* flirter [flurtay]

float *(verb)* flotter [flotay]

floor le sol
on the second floor au deuxième étage [o...ay-tahJ]

flower une fleur [flur]

flu la grippe [greep]

fluide traffic flowing freely
fly *(insect)* la mouche [moosh]
  (go by plane) aller en avion [alay ON av-yON]
foggy: it's foggy il y a du brouillard [eelya dœ broo-yahr]
follow suivre [sweevr]
food la nourriture [nooree-tœr]
  to buy some food acheter à manger [ashtay ah MONJay]
food poisoning une intoxication alimentaire [ANtoxee-kass-yON alee-mON-tair]
fool un/une imbécile [ANbayseel]
foot le pied [p-yay]

✈ 1 foot = 30.5 cm = 0.3 metres

football *(game)* le football
  (ball) un ballon de football [balON...]
for pour [poor]
  that's for me c'est pour moi [seh...mwa]
  I've been here for a week je suis ici *depuis* une semaine [Juh swee zee-see duh-pwee...]
forbidden interdit [ANtair-dee]
foreign étranger [aytrON-Jay]
foreign currency des devises [duh-veez]
foreigner un étranger [aytrON-Jay]
  (woman) une étrangère [aytrON-Jair]
forest une forêt [foreh]
forget oublier [ooblee-yay]
  I forget j'oublie [Jooblee]
  I've forgotten j'ai oublié [Jay ooblee-yay]
  don't forget n'oubliez pas [nooblee-yay pa]
fork *(to eat with)* une fourchette [foor-shet]
form *(document)* un formulaire [formœ-lair]
fortnight une quinzaine [kANzen]
forward *(move etc)* en avant [ON na-vON]
  could you forward my mail? est-ce que vous pouvez faire suivre mon courrier? [eskuh voo

poovay fair sweevr mON koor-yay]

forwarding address l'adresse pour faire suivre le
courrier [ad-ress poor faire sweevr luh koor-yay]

foundation cream le fond de teint [fON duh tAN]

fountain une fontaine [fON-ten]

four-wheel drive un quatre-quatre [katr-katr]

fracture une fracture [frak-tœr]

fragile fragile [fra-Jeel]

France la France [frONss]

fraud une escroquerie [eskrokree]

free libre [leebr]
  (no charge) gratuit [gratwee]
  admission free entrée gratuite [ONtray gratweet]

frein moteur engage low gear

French français [frON-seh]
  I don't speak French je ne parle pas français
  [Juh nuh parl pa...]

Frenchman un Français [frON-seh]

Frenchwoman une Française [frON-sez]

fresh frais/fraîche [freh/fresh]

freshen up: I'd like to freshen up j'aimerais
faire un brin de toilette [Jemreh fair AN brAN duh
twa-let]

Friday vendredi [vONdruh-dee]

fridge un frigo [freego]

fried egg un œuf sur le plat [urf sœr luh pla]

friend un ami [a-mee]
  (female) une amie [a-mee]

friendly sympathique [sANpa-teek]

fries des frites [freet]

from de [duh]
  where is it from? d'où est-ce que ça vient?
  [doo eskuh sa v-yAN]

> **De**, used with **le** becomes **du**. With the
> plural **les** it becomes **des**.
>   **from the centre** du centre

front: in front of you devant toi [duh-VON...]
  at the front devant
frost le gel [Jel]
frostbite des gelures [Juh-lɶr]
fruit des fruits [frwee]
fruit salad une macédoine de fruits [massay-
  dwahn duh frwee]
fry frire [freer]
  nothing fried pas de fritures [pa duh free-tɶr]
frying pan une poêle [pwahl]
full plein [plAN]
fumeurs smoking
fun: it's fun c'est amusant [set amoo-ZON]
  have fun! amusez-vous bien! [amoozay-voo b-yAN]
funny drôle [drol]
furniture les meubles [murbl]
further plus loin [ploo lwAN]
fuse un fusible [foo-zeebl]
future l'avenir [av-neer]
  in future à l'avenir

G [jay]

gale une tempête [toN-pet]
gallon un gallon [galoN]

✈ 1 gallon = 4.55 litres

gallstone un calcul biliaire [kal-kool beel-yair]
gamble jouer [joo-ay]
gambling le jeu [Juh]
garage *(for repairs, parking)* un garage [garahJ]
  (for petrol) une station service [stass-yON sair-
  veess]
garden le jardin [JardAN]
garlic l'ail [I]
gas le gaz [gaz]
  (petrol) de l'essence [ay-soNss]

gas cylinder une bouteille de gaz [boo-tay...]
gasket un joint [JWAN]
gay gay
gear *(in car)* la vitesse [vee-tess]
  (equipment) le matériel [matayr-yel]
  I can't get it into gear je n'arrive pas à passer
  la vitesse [Juh nareev pa ah pa-say...]
gents les toilettes (pour messieurs) [twa-let (poor
  mays-yuh)]
German allemand/allemande [al-moN/al-moNd]
Germany l'Allemagne [al-man-yuh]
gesture un geste [Jest]
get: will you get me a...? est-ce que vous
  pouvez m'*apporter* un/une...? [eskuh voo poovay maportay...]
  how do I get to...? comment est-ce qu'on peut
  aller à...? [komoN eskoN puh alay ah]
  where do I get a bus for...? où est-ce qu'il faut
  prendre le bus pour aller à...? [weskeel fo proNdr
  luh booss pour alay ah...]
  when can I get it back? quand est-ce que
  je peux le récupérer? [koNteskuh Juh puh luh
  raykoopayray]
  when do we get back? quand est-ce que nous
  rentrons? [...roN-troN]
  where do I get off? où est-ce que je dois
  descendre? [weskuh Juh dwa day-soNdr]
  have you got...? avez-vous...? [avay-voo]
  (familiar) as-tu...? [ah-too]
gin du gin [dJeen]
gin and tonic un gin-tonic
girl une fille [fee]
  (young woman) une jeune fille [Jurn...]
girlfriend la petite amie [puhteet a-mee]
gîtes d'étape dormitory accommodation (for
  hikers etc)
gîtes ruraux self-catering accommodation

give donner [donay]

will you give me...? est-ce que vous pouvez me donner...? [eskuh voo poovay muh...]

I gave it to him je le lui ai donné [Juh luh lwee ay donay]

glad content [koN-toN]

glass le verre [vair]

a glass of water un verre d'eau

glasses les lunettes [loo-net]

glue de la colle [kol]

go aller [alay]

when does the bus go? quand est-ce que le bus part? [koNt eskuh luh booss par]

the bus has gone le bus est parti [...eh partee]

he's gone il est parti [eeleh...]

where are you going? où allez-vous? [oo alay voo]

does this go to the airport? c'est bien ça pour aller à l'aéroport? [seh b-yAN sa poor alay ah...]

let's go allons-y [aloN zee]

go on! vas-y! [va-zee]

can I have a go? est-ce que je peux essayer? [eskuh Juh puh esay-yay]

Here is the present tense of the French verb for 'to go'.

I go je vais [Juh veh]
you go *(familiar)* tu vas [too va]
you go *(polite)* vous allez [voo zal-ay]
he/she/it goes il/elle va
we go nous allons [noo zaloN]
you go *(plural)* vous allez
they go ils/elles vont [eel/el voN]

---

goal un but [boot]

God dieu [d-yuh]

goggles *(for skiing)* des lunettes protectrices [loo-net protek-treess]

gold l'or

golf le golf

good bon [bON]

  good! très bien! [treh b-yAN]

goodbye au revoir! [o ruh-vwahr]

got: have you got...? est-ce que vous avez...? [eskuh voo zavay]

  (familiar) est-ce que tu as...? [...too ah]

gram un gramme [gram]

granddaughter la petite-fille [puhteet-fee]

grandfather le grand-père [grON-pair]

grandmother la grand-mère [grON-mair]

grandson le petit-fils [puhtee-feess]

grapefruit un pamplemousse [pONpluh-mooss]

grapefruit juice un jus de pamplemousse [Joo duh pONpluh-mooss]

grapes du raisin [reh-zAN]

grass l'herbe [airb]

grateful: I'm very grateful to you je vous suis très reconnaissant/reconaissante [Juh voo swee treh ruhkoneh-sON/ruhkoneh-sONt]

gratuit free

gravy la sauce [sohss]

grease la graisse [gress]

greasy graisseux [gress-uh]

great grand [grON]

  (very good) fantastique [fONtasteek]

  great! génial! [Jayn-yal]

Greece la Grèce [gress]

greedy avide [aveed]

  (for food) gourmand [goormON]

green vert [vair]

grey gris [gree]

grocer's une épicerie [aypeess-ree]

ground la terre [tair]

on the ground par terre
on the ground floor au rez-de-chaussée [rayd-sho-say]
group un groupe [groop]
  our group leader notre accompagnateur [akONpan-yatur]
  (woman) notre accompagnatrice [akONpan-yatreess]
  I'm with the English group je suis avec le groupe des Anglais [Juh swee...]
guarantee une garantie [garON-tee]
  is there a guarantee? est-ce qu'il y a une garantie? [eskeelya...]
guest un invité [ANvee-tay]
  (woman) une invitée [ANvee-tay]
  (in hotel) un client [klee-yON]
  (woman) une cliente [klee-yONT]
guesthouse une pension [pONss-yON]
guide un/une guide [gheed]
guidebook un guide [gheed]
guided tour une visite guidée [veezeet gheeday]
guilty coupable [koo-pahbl]
guitar la guitare [ghee-tar]
gum *(in mouth)* la gencive [JON-seev]
gun *(pistol)* un revolver [rayvol-vair]

H [ash]

hair les cheveux [shuh-vuh]
hairbrush une brosse à cheveux [bross ah shuh-vuh]
haircut: where can I get a haircut? où est-ce que je peux me faire couper les cheveux? [weskuh Juh puh muh fair koopay lay shuh-vuh]
hairdresser's un coiffeur [kwafur]
hair grip une pince à cheveux [pANss ah shuvuh]
half la moitié [mwat-yay]

a half portion une demi-portion [duh-mee porss-YON]

half an hour une demi-heure [duh-mee ur]
go to **time**

ham du jambon [JON-bON]

hamburger un hamburger [ONbur-gur]

hammer un marteau [marto]

hand la main [MAN]

handbag un sac à main [... ah MAN]

hand baggage les bagages à main [bagahJ ah MAN]

handbrake le frein à main [frAN ah MAN]

handkerchief un mouchoir [moo-shwahr]

handle la poignée [pwan-yay]

handmade fait à la main [feh ah la MAN]

handsome beau/belle [bo/bel]

hanger un cintre [sANtr]

hangover une gueule de bois [gurl duh bwa]

happen arriver [aree-vay]

I don't know how it happened je ne sais pas comment c'est arrivé [...komON seh taree-vay]

what's happening? qu'est-ce qui se passe? [keskee suh pass]

what's happened? qu'est-ce qui s'est passé? [keskee seh pa-say]

happy heureux [ur-ruh]

harbour le port [por]

hard dur [dœr]

hard-boiled egg un œuf dur [urt dœr]

harm le mal

hat un chapeau [sha-po]

hate: I hate... je déteste... [Juh day-test]

have avoir [avwahr]

can I have...? est-ce que je peux avoir [eskuh Juh puh...]

can I have some water? est-ce que je peux avoir de l'eau?

I have no... je n'ai pas de... [Juh nay pa duh...]
do you have any cigars/a map? est-ce que vous avez des cigares/une carte? [eskuh voo zavay...]
I have to leave tomorrow je dois partir demain [Juh dwah...]
do I have to? est-ce qu'il le faut? [eskeel luh fo]

Here is the present tense of the French verb for 'to have'.

I have j'ai [Jay]
you have *(familiar)* tu as [too ah]
you have *(polite)* vous avez [voo zavay]
he/she/it has il/elle a [eel/el ah]
we have nous avons [noo zavON]
you have *(plural)* vous avez
they have ils/elles ont [eel/el zON]

---

hay fever le rhume des foins [room day fwAN]
he il [eel]
head la tête [tet]
headache un mal de tête [mal duh tet]
headlight le phare [far]
head waiter le maître d'hôtel [metr doh-tel]
head wind un vent contraire [vON kON-trair]
health la santé [sON-tay]
  your health! à votre santé [ah votr...]
hear: I can't hear je n'entends pas [Juh nON-tON pa]
hearing aid un sonotone® [sonoton]
heart le cœur [kur]
heart attack une crise cardiaque [kreez kard-yak]
heat la chaleur [shalur]
heating le chauffage [sho-fahJ]
heat stroke un coup de chaleur [koo duh shalur]
heavy lourd [loor]
heel le talon [talON]

could you put new heels on these? est-ce que vous pouvez changer les talons? [eskuh voo poovay sHONJay lay talON]

height la hauteur [o-tur]
(person's) la taille [tɪ]

hello bonjour [bON-Joor]
(in the evening) bonsoir [bON-swahr]
(on phone) allo

help l'aide [ed]
can you help me? est-ce que vous pouvez m'aider? [eskuh voo poovay may-day]
help! au secours! [o suh-koor]

her¹: I know her je *la* connais
will you give it to her? pouvez-vous le *lui* donner? [...lwee...]
with/for her avec/pour elle [...el]
it's her c'est elle [seh tel]
who? – her qui? – elle

her² *(possessive)* son/sa [sON...]
(plural) ses [say]

> Use **son** or **sa** depending on whether the word following takes **le** or **la**.
> **her bag** son sac
> **her suitcase** sa valise
>
> **Son** and **sa** can also mean 'his'. If you need to make things clear you can say:
> **her suitcase** sa valise à elle

here ici [ee-see]
come here venez ici [vuh-nay...]

hers le sien/la sienne [luh see-yAN/la see-yen]
(plural) les siens/les siennes [lay see-yAN/lay see-yen]
it's hers c'est à elle [seh ta el]

hi! salut! [salœ]
(to a person you don't know) bonjour [bON-Joor]

high haut [o]
  higher up plus haut [plœ o]
high chair une chaise haute [shez oht]
hill une colline [koleen]
  (on road) une côte [koht]
him: I know him je *le* connais [...luh...]
  will you give it to him? pouvez-vous le *lui* donner? [...lwee...]
  with/for him avec/pour lui
  it's him c'est lui
  who him qui? – lui
hire *go to* **rent**
his son/sa [SON...]
  (plural) ses [say]

> Use **son** or **sa** depending on whether the word following takes **le** or **la**.
>   **his bag** son sac
>   **his suitcase** sa valise
>
> **Son** and **sa** can also mean 'her'. If you need to make things clear you can say:
>   **his suitcase** sa valise à lui [...ah lwee]

---

  his is... le sien/la sienne est ... [luh see-yAN/la see-yen...]
  his are... les siens/les siennes sont... [lay see-yAN/lay see-yen...]
  it's his c'est à lui
hit: he hit me il m'a frappé [eel ma frapay]
hitch-hike faire du stop [fair dœ...]
hitch-hiker un auto-stoppeur [oto-stopur]
  (female) une auto-stoppeuse [oto-stopurz]
hitch-hiking le stop
hold *(verb)* tenir [tuh-neer]
hole un trou [troo]
holiday les vacances [vakONss]
  (single day) un jour de congé [Joor duh kONjay]

I'm on holiday je suis en vacances [Juh swee zoN...]

Holland la Hollande [oloNd]

home la maison [mezoN]

  at home chez moi [shay mwa]

  (back in Britain) chez nous [...noo]

  I want to go home je veux rentrer chez moi [Juh vuh roNtray...]

homesick: I'm homesick j'ai le mal du pays [Jay luh mal doo payee]

hommes men

honest honnête [onet]

honestly? vraiment? [vreh-moN]

honey du miel [mee-yel]

honeymoon la lune de miel [loon duh mee-yel]

hope l'espoir [espwahr]

  I hope that... j'espère que... [Jespair kuh]

  I hope so j'espère que oui [...wee]

  I hope not j'espère que non [...noN]

horn *(of car)* le klaxon

horodateur pay-and-display (ticket machine)

horrible horrible [oreebl]

horse un cheval [shuh-val]

hospital un hôpital [opee-tal]

> ✈ You'll have to pay for treatment and then, using your E111 (which you get from a UK post office), claim a partial refund.

host l'hôte [oht]

hostess l'hôtesse [o-tess]

hot chaud [sho]

  (spiced) épicé [aypee-say]

  I'm so hot! j'ai tellement chaud! [Jay telmoN...]

  it's so hot today! il fait tellement chaud aujourd'hui! [eel feh...oJoordwee]

hotel un hôtel [otel]

  at my hotel dans mon hôtel [doN...]

> ✈ Price is per room unless otherwise specified.
>   Breakfast will be extra.

hôtel de ville town hall
hour une heure [ur]
house une maison [mezON]
how comment [komON]
   how many? combien? [kONb-yAN]
   how much? combien?
   how much is it? c'est combien? [seh...]
   how long does it take? combien de temps est-
   ce qu'il faut? [kONb-yAN duh tON eskeel fo]
   how long have you been here? vous êtes ici
   depuis combien de temps? [voo zet ee-see duh-
   pwee...]
   how are you? comment allez-vous? [komON
   talay-voo]

> *YOU MAY THEN HEAR*
> très bien merci *very well thanks*
> comme ci, comme ça *so-so*

humid humide [∞-meed]
hungry: I'm hungry j'ai faim [Jay fAN]
   I'm not hungry je n'ai pas faim [Juh nay pa...]
hurry: I'm in a hurry je suis pressé [Juh swee
   pressay]
   please hurry! dépêchez-vous [daypeshay-voo]
hurt: it hurts ça fait mal [sa feh...]
   my leg hurts j'ai mal à la jambe [Jay mal ah...]
husband le mari [ma-ree]

I [ee]

I je [Juh]
ice de la glace [glass]
   with lots of ice avec beaucoup de glace [ah-vek
   bo-koo...]

ice-axe le piolet [pee-olay]

ice cream une glace [glass]

iced coffee un café glacé [kafay glassay]

identity papers les papiers d'identité [pap-yay deedON-tee-tay]

idiot un/une imbécile [ANbayseel]

if si [see]

ignition *(of car)* l'allumage [alω-mahJ]

ill malade [ma-lad]
  I feel ill je ne me sens pas bien [Juh nuh muh sON pa b-yAN]

illegal illégal [eelay-gal]

illegible illisible [eelee-zeebl]

illness une maladie [mala-dee]

immediately tout de suite [toot sweet]

important important [ANpor-TON]
  it's very important c'est très important [seh trehz...]

impossible impossible [ANposseebl]

impressive remarquable [ruhmar-kahbl]

improve améliorer [amayl-yoray]
  I want to improve my French je veux améliorer mon français [Juh vuh amayl-yoray mON frON-seh]

in dans [dON]
  in England en Angleterre [ON...]
  in Glasgow à Glasgow [ah...]
  in 1982 en 1982 [ON...]
  is he in? est-ce qu'il est là? [eskeelh la]

inch un pouce [pooss]

  ✈ 1 inch = 2.54 cm

include inclure [AN-klωr]
  does that include breakfast? est-ce que le petit déjeuner est compris? [eskuh luh puhtee dayJurnay eh kONpree]

incompetent incompétent [ANkON-pay-tON]

inconsiderate: he was inconsiderate il a
manqué d'égards [eel ah moN-kay day-gar]
incredible incroyable [ANkrwy-yahbl]
indecent indécent [ANday-soN]
independent indépendant [ANday-poN-doN]
India l'Inde [ANd]
indicate: he turned without indicating il a
tourné sans *mettre le clignotant* [...soN metr luh
kleen-yotoN]
(cyclist) il a tourné sans le signaler [...seen-yalay]
indicator *(on car)* le clignotant [kleen-yotoN]
indigestion l'indigestion [ANdee-Jest-yoN]
indoors à l'intérieur [ah lANtayr-yur]
infection une infection [ANfeks-yoN]
infectious contagieux [koNtahJ-yuh]
information des informations [ANfor-mass-yoN]
do you have any information in English on...?
est-ce que vous avez des informations en anglais
sur...? [eskuh voo zavay...oN noN-gleh soor]
is there an information office? est-ce qu'il y
a un bureau de renseignements? [eskeelya AN
booro duh roNsayn-yuh-moN]
injection une piqûre [pee-koor]
injured blessé [blessay]
injury une blessure [blessoor]
innocent innocent [eeno-soN]
insect un insecte [AN-sekt]
insect repellent une crème anti-insecte [krem
oN-tee-]
inside à l'intérieur [ah lANtayr-yur]
insist: I insist j'insiste [JANseest]
insomnia l'insomnie [ANsom-nee]
instant coffee du café soluble [kafay soloobl]
instead à la place [ah la plass]
instead of... au lieu de... [o l-yuh duh]
insulating tape du chatterton [shaturtoN]
insult une insulte [ANsoolt]

insurance une assurance [asœ-roNss]
insurance company la compagnie d'assurances
[...koNpan-yee dasœ-roNss]
intelligent intelligent [ANtay-lee-JON]
interdit forbidden
interdit aux piétons no pedestrians
interesting intéressant [ANtay-ressoN]
international international [ANtair-nass-yonal]
Internet l'Internet [ANtairnet]
Internet café un cybercafé [seebair-kafay]
interpret interpréter [ANtair-praytay]
  would you interpret for us? est-ce que vous
  pouvez nous servir d'interprète? [eskuh voo
  poovay noo sair-veer dANtair-pret]
interpreter l'interprète [ANtair-pret]
into dans [doN]
  I'm not into that c'est pas mon truc [seh pa
  moN trook]
introduce: can I introduce...? puis-je vous
  présenter...? [pweeJ voo prayzoN-tay]
invalid *(disabled)* un/une invalide [ANvaleed]
invitation une invitation [ANvee-tass-yoN]
  thanks for the invitation merci pour votre
  invitation [mairsee poor votr...]
invite: can I invite you out? puis-je vous inviter
  à sortir? [pweeJ voo zANvee-tay ah sorteer]
Ireland l'Irlande [eer-loND]
Irish irlandais/irlandaise [eerloN-deh/eerloN-dez]
iron *(for clothes)* un fer à repasser [fair ah ruhpasay]
  will you iron these for me? pouvez-vous me
  repasser ceci [poovay-voo muh ruhpasay suh-see]
is *go to* **be**
island une île [eel]
it: I'll take it je le/la prends
  it is... c'est... [seh]
  it's him c'est lui
  is it...? est-ce que c'est...? [eskuh seh]

where is it? *(place etc)* où est-ce que c'est?
[weskuh seh]
(a particular object) où est-ce qu'il/elle est?
[weskeel/el eh]
  it's not working ça ne marche pas [sa...]
Italian italien/italienne [eetal-YAN/eetal-yen]
Italy l'Italie [eetalee]
itch: it itches ça démange [sa day-MONJ]
itemize: would you itemize it for me? est-ce
  que vous pouvez me *faire une facture détaillée?*
  [eskuh voo poovay muh fair œn fak-tœr daytI-yay]

J [Jee]

jack *(for car)* un cric [kreek]
jacket une veste [vest]
jam de la confiture [kONfee-tœr]
  traffic jam un embouteillage [ONboo-tay-yahJ]
January janvier [JONv-yay]
jaw la mâchoire [mash-wahr]
jealous jaloux [Jaloo]
jeans le jean [dJeen]
jellyfish une méduse [may-dœz]
jetty la jetée [Juh-tay]
jewellery des bijoux [bee-Joo]
job un travail [tra-vI]
  just the job parfait [parfeh]
joke une blague [blag]
  you must be joking! vous plaisantez! [voo
  plezON-tay]
jour de fermeture... closed on...
jours fériés public holidays
journey le voyage [vwy-ahJ]
  have a good journey! bon voyage! [bON...]
July juillet [Jwee-yeh]
junction le croisement [krwaz-mON]
  (on motorway) la sortie [sortee]

June juin [JWAN]
junk du bric à brac [breeka-brak]
  (food) des cochonneries [koshonuhree]
just *(only)* juste [JOOst]]
  (exactly) exactement [eg-zaktuhmON]
  just two deux seulement [...surlmON]
  just there juste là
  just a little juste un petit peu [...AN puhtee puh]
  just now pour l'instant [poor lANstON]
  not just now pas pour l'instant
  he was here just now il était là à l'instant [eel
  ayteh la ah...]
  that's just right ça va très bien [sa va treh b-
  yAN]

K [ka]

keep: can I keep it? est-ce que je peux le/la
  garder? [eskuh Juh puh luh/la garday]
  keep the change gardez la monnaie [garday la
  moneh]
  you didn't keep your promise vous n'avez pas
  tenu votre promesse [voo navay pa tuh-nOO votr
  promess]
  it keeps on breaking ça se casse tout le temps
  [sass kass too luh tON]
key une clé [klay]
keycard une carte-clé [kart-klay]
kidney le rein [rAN]
  (food) le rognon [ron-yON]
kill tuer [tOO-ay]
kilo un kilo

> ✈ kilos/5 x 11 = pounds

kilos	1	1.5	5	6	7	8	9
pounds	2.2	3.3	11	13.2	15.4	17.6	19.8

kilometre un kilomètre [keelo-metr]

✈ kilometres/8 x 5 = miles

kilometres	1	5	10	20	50	100
miles	0.62	3.11	6.2	12.4	31	62

kind: that's very kind of you c'est très *aimable*
de votre part [seh treh zeh-mahbl duh votr par]
what kind of...? quelle sorte de...? [kel sort duh]
kiss un baiser [bezzay]
(verb) embrasser [ONbrassay]

✈ A quick peck or several on the cheeks (**une bise**) is a common form of greeting female/ female and female/male between family and friends.

kitchen la cuisine [kwee-zeen]
knee le genou [Juh-noo]
knife un couteau [kooto]
knock *(verb: at door)* frapper [frapay]
  there's a knocking noise from the engine il y
  a le moteur qui cogne [eelya luh mo-tur kee kon-
  yuh]
know savoir [savwahr]
  (person, place) connaître [konetr]
  I don't know je ne sais pas [Juh nuh seh pa]
  I didn't know je ne savais pas [...saveh pa]
  I don't know the area je ne connais pas la
  région [Juh nuh koneh pa...]

L [el]

label l'étiquette [aytee-ket]
laces des lacets [lasseh]
lacquer de la laque [lak]
ladies (toilet) les toilettes (pour dames) [twa-let
  (poor dam)]
lady une dame [dam]
lager une bière (blonde) [bee-yair...]

✈ Lager and lime is not common. But if you want a mix, try **un demi-pêche** (with peach syrup), **un demi-cassis** (with black-currant) or **un Monaco** (with grenadine).

lake le lac
lamb *(meat)* de l'agneau [an-yo]
lamp une lampe [loNp]
lamppost un lampadaire [loNpa-dair]
lampshade un abat-jour [aba-Joor]
land la terre [tair]
lane *(on road)* la voie [vwa]
language la langue [loNg]
language course un cours de langue [koor duh loNg]
laptop un (ordinateur) portable [(ordeenatur) portahbl]
large grand [groN]
laryngitis une laryngite [larAN-Jeet]
last dernier [dairn-yay]
  last year l'année dernière [lanay dairn-yair]
  last week la semaine dernière [suh-men...]
  last night hier soir [yair swahr]
  (during the night) la nuit dernière [la nwee dairn-yair]
  at last! enfin! [ONfAN]
late tard [tar]
  sorry I'm late désolé, je suis *en retard* [dayzolay Juh swee zON ruh-tar]
  it's a bit late il est un peu tard [eeleh AN puh...]
  please hurry, I'm late dépêchez-vous, s'il vous plaît, je suis en retard [day-peshay-voo seel voo pleh Juh swee...]
  at the latest au plus tard [o pl∞...]
later plus tard [pl∞ tar]
  see you later à tout à l'heure [ah toota lur]
laugh *(verb)* rire [reer]

launderette une laverie automatique [lav-ree oto-ma-teek]

lavatory les toilettes [twa-let]

law la loi [lwa]

lawyer un avocat [ahvo-ka]
(woman) une avocate [ahvo-kat]

laxative un laxatif [laxa-teef]

lay-by une aire de stationnement [air duh stass-yon-moN]

lazy paresseux [paressuh]

leaf une feuille [fuh-ee]

leak une fuite [fweet]
  it leaks ça fuit [sa fwee]

learn: I want to learn... je veux apprendre... [Juh vuh aproNdr]

lease *(verb)* louer [loo-ay]

least: not in the least pas du tout [pa doo too]
  at least au moins [o mwaN]

leather du cuir [kweer]

leave *(go away)* partir [parteer]
  we're leaving tomorrow nous partons demain [noo partoN duh-maN]
  when does the bus leave? quand est-ce que le bus part? [koNteskuh...par]
  I left two shirts in my room j'ai laissé deux chemises dans ma chambre [Jay lessay...]
  can I leave this here? est-ce que je peux laisser ça ici? [eskuh Juh puh lessay sa ee-see]

left gauche [gohsh]
  on the left à gauche [ah...]

left-handed gaucher [go-shay]

left luggage (office) la consigne [koN-seen-yuh]

leg la jambe [JoNb]

legal légal [lay-gal]

lemon un citron [see-troN]

lemonade de la limonade [leemo-nad]

lend: will you lend me your...? est-ce que vous

pouvez me *prêter* votre...? [eskuh voo poovay
muh preh-tay votr]

lens *(for camera)* l'objectif [obɹek-teef]
  (of glasses) le verre [vair]

less moins [mwaN]
  less than that moins que ça [...kuh sa]

let: let me help *laissez-moi* vous aider [lessay-
mwa voo zay-day]
  let me go! laissez-moi!
  will you let me off here? est-ce que vous
pouvez me laisser descendre ici? [eskuh voo
poovay muh lessay day-soNdr ee-see]
  let's go allons-y [aloNz-ee]

letter une lettre [letr]
  are there any letters for me? est-ce qu'il y a
du courrier pour moi? [eskeelya dœ koor-yay
poor mwa]

letterbox une boîte aux lettres [bwat o letr]

lettuce une salade [sa-lad]

level-crossing le passage à niveau [pa-sahɹ ah
neevo]

liable *(responsible)* responsable [respoN-sahbl]

librairie bookshop

library la bibliothèque [beeblee-o-tek]

libre vacant; free

libre service self-service

licence un permis [pairmee]

lid le couvercle [koo-vairkl]

lie *(untruth)* un mensonge [moN soNɹ]
  can he lie down for a bit? est-ce qu'il peut
s'étendre un moment? [eskeel puh say-toNdr AN
momoN]

life la vie [vee]
  that's life c'est la vie [seh...]

lifebelt la bouée de sauvetage [boo-ay duh sohv-
tahɹ]

lifeboat le canot de sauvetage [ka-no duh sohv-tahJ]

life-guard le maître nageur sauveteur [metr na-Jur sohv-tur]

life insurance une assurance-vie [asoo-rONss-vee]

life jacket le gilet de sauvetage [Jeeleh duh sohv-tahJ]

lift: do you want a lift? est-ce que je peux vous déposer? [eskuh Juh puh voo day-pozay]

could you give me a lift? est-ce que vous pouvez me déposer? [eskuh voo poovay muh...]

the lift isn't working l'ascenseur ne marche pas [lasON-sur nuh marsh pa]

light *(not heavy)* léger [lay-Jay]

(not dark) clair [klair]

the lights aren't working la lumière ne s'allume pas [la loom-yair nuh saloom pa]

(of car) les phares ne s'allument pas [lay far nuh saloom pa]

have you got a light? est-ce que vous avez du feu? [eskuh voo zavay doo fuh]

light blue bleu clair

light bulb une ampoule [ON-pool]

lighter un briquet [breekeh]

like: would you like...? est-ce que vous voulez...? [eskuh voo voolay]

I'd like a... j'aimerais un/une... [Jemreh...]

I'd like to... j'aimerais...

I like it ça me plaît [sa muh pleh]

I like you je vous aime bien [Juh voo zem b-yAN]

(romantic) vous me plaisez [voo muh plezzay]

I like him/her je l'aime bien

I don't like it ça ne me plaît pas [sa nuh muh pleh pa]

what's it like? c'est comment? [seh komON]

do it like this faites comme ça [fet kom sa]

one like that un comme ça [AN kom sa]

lime un citron vert [seetrON vair]

lime juice un jus de citron vert [J∞ duh seetrON vair]

line la ligne [leen-yuh]

lip la lèvre [levr]

lip salve du baume à lèvres [bohm ah levr]

lipstick du rouge à lèvres [rooJ ah levr]

liqueur une liqueur [lee-kur]

list une liste [leest]

listen écouter [aykoo-tay]

   listen! écoutez! [aykoo-tay]

litre un litre [leetr]

> ✈ 1 litre = 1.75 pints = 0.22 gals

little petit [puhtee]

   a little ice un peu de glace [AN puh duh...]

   a little more un peu plus [...pl∞ss]

   just a little juste un petit peu [J∞st...]

live habiter [abeetay]

   (be alive) vivre [veevr]

   I live in Glasgow j'habite à Glasgow [Jabeet ah...]

   where do you live? où est-ce que vous habitez? [weskuh voo zabeetay]

liver le foie [fwa]

lizard le lézard [layzar]

loaf un pain [pAN]

lobster une langouste [lON-goost]

local: could we try a local wine? on pourrait essayer un vin *de la région*? [ON pooreh esay-yay un vAN duh la rayJ-yON]

   a local restaurant un restaurant du coin [...d∞ kwAN]

location de voitures car rental

lock: the lock's broken la *serrure* est cassée [la say-r∞r eh ka-say]

   I've locked myself out je me suis enfermé dehors [Juh muh swee ONfair-may duh-or]

London Londres [loNdr]

lonely seul [surl]

long long [loN]

we'd like to stay longer nous aimerions rester plus longtemps [nooz em-uh-ree-yoN restay ploo loN-toN]

a long time longtemps

loo: where's the loo? où sont les toilettes? [oo soN lay twa-let]

look: you look tired vous *avez l'air* fatigué [voo zavay lair...]

look at that regardez ça [ruhgar-day sa]

can I have a look? est-ce que je peux regarder? [eskuh Juh puh ruhgar-day]

I'm just looking je regarde [Juh ruh-gard]

will you look after my bags? pouvez-vous surveiller mes sacs? [poovay-voo soorvay-yay...]

I'm looking for... je cherche... [Juh shairsh]

look out! attention! [atoNss-yoN]

loose *(undone)* défait [day-feh]

(clothes) ample [oNpl]

lorry un camion [kam-yoN]

lorry driver un chauffeur de camion [sho-fur duh kam-yoN]

lose perdre [pairdr]

I've lost... j'ai perdu... [Jay pairdoo...]

excuse me, I'm lost pardon monsieur/ madame, je suis perdu [...Juh swee...]

lost property (office) le bureau des objets trouvés [booro day zob-Jeh troovay]

lot: a lot beaucoup [bo-koo]

not a lot pas beaucoup [pa...]

a lot of chips beaucoup de frites

a lot more expensive beaucoup plus cher [...ploo shair]

lotion une lotion [lohss-yoN]

loud fort [for]

it's too loud c'est trop fort [seh tro...]
louder plus fort [ploo...]
louer: à louer to let
lounge *(in house, hotel)* le salon [salON]
(at airport) le hall
love: I love you je vous aime [Juh voo zem]
(familiar) je t'aime [Juh tem]
do you love me? est-ce que vous m'aimez?
[eskuh voo memay]
he's/she's in love il est amoureux/elle est
amoureuse [eel eh tamoo-ruh/el eh tamoo-rurz]
I love this wine j'adore ce vin [Jador suh vAN]
lovely beau/belle [bo/bel]
(view etc) très joli [treh Jolee]
(meal etc) délicieux [dayleess-yuh]
low bas [ba]
luck la chance [shONss]
good luck! bonne chance! [bon...]
lucky: you're lucky vous avez de la chance [voo
zavay duh la shONss]
that's lucky! quelle chance! [kel...]
luggage les bagages [bagahJ]
lunch le déjeuner [day-Jurnay]

✈ In Switzerland and Belgium **déjeuner** is
commonly used for 'breakfast'. Use **dîner**
[deenay] for 'lunch'.

lungs les poumons [poomON]
luxury le luxe [lɔɔx]

M [em]

mad fou/folle [foo/fol]
made-to-measure fait sur mesure [feh sɔɔr muh-
zɔɔr]
magazine un magazine
magnificent magnifique [man-yee-feek]

maid la femme de chambre [fam duh shONbr]

maiden name le nom de jeune fille [NON duh Jurn fee]

mail le courrier [koor-yay]

  is there any mail for me? est-ce qu'il y a du courrier pour moi? [eskeelya dœ....poor mwa]

main road la rue principale [rœ praNseepal]

  (in the country) la grande route [grOND root]

make faire [fair]

  will we make it in time? est-ce qu'on y arrivera à temps? [eskON nee areev-ra ah tON]

make-up le maquillage [makee-yahJ]

man un homme [om]

  the man in reception le monsieur à la reception [luh muhs-yuh...]

manager le directeur [deerek-tur]

  (woman) la directrice [deerek-treess]

  can I see the manager? j'aimerais parler au directeur [Jemreh parlay o...]

many beaucoup [bo-koo]

  many... beaucoup de... [...duh]

map une carte [kart]

  (of city) un plan [plON]

  a map of Paris un plan de Paris [AN plON duh pa-ree]

March mars [marss]

marina le port de plaisance [por duh plezONss]

market le marché [marshay]

marmalade de la confiture d'oranges [kONfee-tœr doroNJ]

married marié [maree-ay]

marry: will you marry me? voulez-vous m'épouser? [voolay-voo maypoo-zay]

marvellous merveilleux [mairvay-yuh]

mascara du mascara

mashed potatoes de la purée de pommes de terre [pœ-ray duh pom duh tair]

mass *(in church)* la messe [mess]

massage un massage [ma-sahJ]

mast le mât [ma]

mat un petit tapis [puhtee tapee]

match: a box of matches une boîte d'*allumettes* [bwat daloo-met]

   a football match un match de football

material *(cloth)* du tissu [tee-soo]

matter: it doesn't matter ça ne fait rien [sa nuh feh ree-yAN]

   what's the matter? qu'est-ce qui ne va pas? [keskee nuh va pa]

mattress un matelas [mat-la]

mature mûr [moor]

maximum le maximum [maxee-mom]

May mai [meh]

may: may I have...? est-ce que je peux avoir...? [eskuh Juh puh avwahr]

maybe peut-être [purt-etr]

mayonnaise de la mayonnaise [ma-yonehz]

me: he knows me il *me* connaît [...muh...]

   please give it to me donnez-le *moi*, s'il vous plaît [donay-luh mwa...]

   with/for me avec/pour moi

   it's me c'est moi [seh...]

   who? – me qui? – moi

meal un repas [ruh-pa]

mean: what does this mean? qu'est-ce que ça veut dire? [keskuh sa vuh deer]

measles la rougeole [roo-Johl]

   German measles la rubéole [roobay-ohl]

measurements les dimensions [deemONss-yON]

meat de la viande [vee-yONd]

mechanic: is there a mechanic here? est-ce qu'il y a un *mécanicien* ici? [eskeelya AN maykaneess-yAN ee-see]

medicine *(for cold etc)* un médicament [maydeekamON]

Mediterranean la Méditerranée [maydee-tairanay]

meet rencontrer [rONkONtray]

pleased to meet you enchanté de faire votre connaissance [ONshON-tay duh fair votr koneh-sONss]

when shall we meet? quand est-ce que nous nous voyons? [kONteskuh noo noo vwy-yON]

meeting une réunion [ray-oon-yON]

melon un melon [muh-lON]

member un membre [mONbr]

how do I become a member? comment est-ce que je peux devenir membre? [komON eskuh Juh puh duhv-neer...]

men les hommes [om]

mend: can you mend this? est-ce que vous pouvez *réparer* ça? [eskuh voo poovay raypa-ray sa]

mention: don't mention it je vous en prie [Juh voo zON pree]

menu la carte [kart]

can I have the menu, please? est-ce que je peux avoir la carte, s'il vous plaît? [eskuh Juh puh avwahr...]

go to pages 84-87

mesdames ladies

mess une pagaille [pag-I]

message un message [messahJ]

(text) un texto

are there any messages for me? est-ce que quelqu'un a laissé un message pour moi? [eskuh kelkAN ah lessay AN...poor mwa]

can I leave a message for...? est-ce que je peux laisser un message pour...? [eskuh Juh puh...]

messieurs men

metre un mètre [metr]

✈ 1 metre = 39.37 inches = 1.09 yds

métro underground

> ✈ The Paris **métro** doesn't have names for the
> different lines. Look for the name of the last
> station on the line and that'll be the direc-
> tion (or **correspondance**) to head for. A
> flat fare applies and you can buy **un carnet**
> (book) of ten tickets.

midday midi [mee-dee]
  at midday à midi
middle le milieu [meel-yuh]
  in the middle au milieu [o...]
Midi South of France
midnight minuit [meen-wee]
might: he might have gone il est peut-être parti
  [eel eh purt-etr...]
migraine une migraine [mee-gren]
mild doux [doo]
mile un 'mile'

> ✈ miles/5 x 8 = kilometres
>
> | miles | 0.5 | 1 | 3 | 5 | 10 | 50 | 100 |
> |---|---|---|---|---|---|---|---|
> | kilometres | 0.8 | 1.6 | 4.8 | 8 | 16 | 80 | 160 |

milk du lait [leh]
  a glass of milk un verre de lait [vair duh...]
milkshake un 'milkshake'
millimetre un millimètre [meelee-metr]
milometer le compteur kilométrique [kON-tur
  keelomay-treek]
mind: I've changed my mind j'ai changé d'avis
  [Jay shONJay da-vee]
  I don't mind ça ne me dérange pas [san muh
  day-rONJ pa]
  (it's all the same) ça m'est égal [sa meh tay-gal]
  do you mind if I...? est-ce que ça vous dérange
  si...? [eskuh sa voo day-rONJ see]
  never mind tant pis [tON pee]

I'd like
j'aimerais
[Jemreh]

water
de l'eau
[duh lo]

bread
du pain
[doo pAN]

beef
du bœuf
[...buhf]

chicken
du poulet
[...pooleh]

lamb
de l'agneau
[...an-yo]

Entrées: Starters

bouchée à la reine vol au vent
crudités selection of salads or chopped raw vegetables
cuisses de grenouille frogs' legs
escargots de Bourgogne à la douzaine a dozen Burgundy snails
macédoine de légumes mixed vegetables with mayonnaise
œufs mimosa egg mayonnaise
rillettes potted pork and goose meat
salade composée mixed salad
salade de gésiers green salad with gizzards
salade niçoise salad with olives, tomatoes, anchovies and hard boiled eggs
terrine du chef pâté maison, chef's special pâté

Potages: Soups

bisque d'écrevisses freshwater crayfish soup
crème de bolets cream of mushroom soup
soupe à l'oignon onion soup
velouté de tomates cream of tomato soup
vichyssoise cold vegetable soup

Viandes: Meat dishes

bifteck steak
cheval horse
confit de canard duck preserve
coq au vin chicken in red wine
côtelette de porc pork chop
dinde turkey
escalope panée breaded veal etc

foie de veau calf's liver
gigot d'agneau leg of lamb
langue de boeuf ox tongue
magret de canard duck breast
paupiettes de veau rolled-up stuffed slice of veal
pintade guinea fowl
porc pork
rognons au madère kidneys in Madeira
steak haché minced meat
steak tartare raw minced beef with a raw egg
tournedos fillet steak
veau veal

Volaille et Gibier: Poultry and Game

canard à l'orange duck in orange sauce
civet de lièvre jugged hare
lapin chasseur rabbit in white wine and herbs
poule chicken
poulet rôti roast chicken

Poissons et marée: fish and seafood

cabillaud cod
coquilles Saint-Jacques scallops
crevettes prawns
fruits de mer seafood
homard à l'américaine lobster with tomato and white wine
huîtres oysters
langouste crayfish
langoustine saltwater crayfish; scampi
morue cod

can I have what he's having?
pourrais-je avoir la même chose que lui?
[poorehJ avwahr la mem shohz kuh lwee]

red wine
du vin rouge
[doo vAN ...]

white wine
du vin blanc
[...blON]

beer
de la bière
[...bee-yair]

moules marinière mussels in white wine

raie au beurre noir skate fried in butter

truite aux amandes trout with almonds

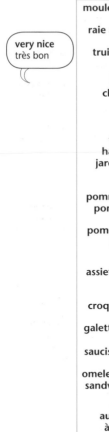

very nice
très bon

Légumes: vegetables

champignons mushrooms

chou cabbage

chou-fleur cauliflower

épinards spinach

frites chips, French fries

haricots verts green beans

jardinière de légumes mixed vegetables

petits pois peas

pommes dauphine potato fritters

pommes de terre à l'anglaise boiled potatoes

pommes frites chips, French fries

purée mashed potatoes

Snacks

assiette anglaise selection of cold meats

crêpe pancake

croque-monsieur toasted cheese sandwich with ham

galette round flat cake; wholemeal pancake

saucisse, frites Frankfurter sausage and chips

omelette au jambon ham omelette

sandwich crudités salad sandwich

Desserts

aux amandes with almonds

à l'ananas with pineapple

aux cerises with cherries
charlotte dessert consisting of layers of fruit, cream and biscuits
au citron with lemon
compote stewed fruit
coulis de framboises raspberry sauce
crème anglaise custard
flan custard tart
glace ice cream
pâtisserie maison homemade gateau
plateau de fromages cheese board
poire belle-Hélène pear in chocolate sauce with ice cream
aux pommes with apples
aux prunes with plums
raisin grapes
sabayon egg yolks and Marsala wine
tarte aux myrtilles bilberry tart
tarte Tatin baked apple dish

Some general terms

à l'ail with garlic
au gratin baked in a milk, cream and cheese sauce
beurre blanc butter sauce
compris included
fait maison homemade
formule express set lunch menu
garni with French fries or rice and/or vegetables
menu set menu
pâtes pasta
plat de résistance main course
plat du jour dish of the day
provençale with tomatoes, garlic and herbs
restauration rapide snack bar

vanilla
à la vanille
[...va-nee]

strawberry
à la fraise
[...frez]

chocolate
au chocolat

coffee
un café

the bill, please
l'addition, s'il vous plaît

mine le mien/la mienne [mee-yAN/mee-yen]
(plural) les miens/les miennes [mee-yAN/mee-yen]
  it's mine c'est à moi [seh ta mwa]
mineral water de l'eau minérale [o meenay-rahl]
minimum le minimum [meenee-mom]
minus moins [mwAN]
  minus 3 degrees moins trois
minute une minute [meenoot]
  in a minute dans un instant [dON zAN ANstON]
  just a minute un instant
mirror un miroir [meer-wahr]
Miss Mademoiselle [mad-mwa-zel]
miss: I miss you vous me manquez [voo muh mON-kay]
  he's missing il a disparu [eel ah deespa-roo]
  there is a... missing il y a un/une... qui manque [eelya AN/oon...kee mONk]
  we missed the bus nous avons raté le bus [noo zavON ratay luh booss]
mist la brume [broom]
mistake une erreur [air-rur]
  I think you've made a mistake je crois que vous vous êtes trompé [Juh krwa kuh voo voo zet trON-pay]
misunderstanding un malentendu [malON-tON-doo]
mobile (phone) un (téléphone) portable [taylay-fon portahbl]
  my mobile number is... mon numéro de portable est le... [mON noomay-ro duh...eh luh]
modern moderne [modairn]
moisturizer une crème hydratante [krem eedra-tONt]
Monday lundi [lAN-dee]
money l'argent [arJON]
  I've lost my money j'ai perdu mon argent [Jay

pairdœ mON...]

I have no money je n'ai pas d'argent [Juh nay pa darJON]

money belt une banane [ba-nan]

month un mois [mwa]

moon la lune [lœn]

moorings les amarres [am-ar]

moped un mobylette [mobee-let]

more plus [plœss]

  can I have some more? est-ce que je peux en avoir plus? [eskuh Juh puh ON navwahr plœss]

  more wine, please encore du vin, s'il vous plaît [ON-kor dœ vAN...]

  no more thanks merci, ça suffit [mair-see sa sœ-fee]

  more than that plus que ça [plœss kuh sa]

  no more money plus d'argent [plœ...]

  I haven't got any more je n'en ai plus [Juh nON nay plœ]

  there aren't any more il n'y en a plus [eeln yON ah plœ]

  more comfortable plus confortable [plœ...]

morning le matin [matAN]

  good morning bonjour (monsieur/madame/ mademoiselle) [bON-Joor muhs-yuh/ma-dam/ mad-mwa-zel]

  in the morning le matin

  (tomorrow) demain matin [duh-mAN...]

  this morning ce matin [suh...]

mosquito un moustique [moosteek]

most: the most le plus [luh plœ]

  I like this one the most c'est celui que je préfère [seh suh-lwee kuh Juh pray-fair]

  most of the people la plupart des gens [plœpar day JON]

mother: my mother ma mère [...mair]

motor le moteur [mo-tur]

motorbike une moto [moto]
motorboat un bateau à moteur [bato ah mo-tur]
motorcyclist un/une motocycliste [moto-see-kleest]
motorist un/une automobiliste [oto-mo-bee-leest]
motorway l'autoroute [oto-root]
mountain une montagne [MON-tan-yuh]
  in the mountains à la montagne
mountaineer un/une alpiniste [alpeeneest]
mountaineering l'alpinisme [alpeeneess-muh]
mouse *(also for computer)* une souris [sooree]
moustache une moustache [moostash]
mouth la bouche [boosh]
move: don't move ne *bougez* pas [nuh boo-Jay pa]
  could you move your car? est-ce que vous pouvez *déplacer* votre voiture? [eskuh voo poovay dayplasay votr vwatoor]
movie un film [feelm]
MPV un monospace [monospass]
Mr Monsieur, M. [muh-syuh]
Mrs Madame, Mme [ma-dam]
Ms Madame, Mme [ma-dam]
much beaucoup [bo-koo]
  much better beaucoup mieux [...m-yuh]
  not much pas beaucoup [pa...]
mug: I've been mugged j'ai été agressé [Jay aytay agressay]
mum: my mum ma mère [...mair]
muscle un muscle [mooskl]
museum le musée [moozay]

✈ Mostly shut on Tuesdays. National museums are free on the first Sunday of each month.

mushrooms des champignons [shONpeen-yON]

music la musique [mɔozeek]
must: I must have a... je dois avoir un/une...
  [Juh dwa zavwahr...]
  I must not eat... je ne dois pas manger...
  you must do it vous devez le faire [voo duh-vay...]
  you mustn't... vous ne devez pas...

> A common way of expressing 'must' is
> with **il faut** [eel fo].
>   **I must be going** il faut que je m'en aille
>   **no, I/you must** non, il le faut
>   **you mustn't do that** il ne faut pas faire
>   cela

mustard de la moutarde [mootard]
my mon/ma [moN/ma]
  (plural) mes [may]

> Use **mon** or **ma** depending on whether
> the word following takes **le** or **la**.
>   **my husband/my wife** mon mari/ma
>   femme

N [en]

nail *(on finger)* un ongle [ONgl]
  (for wood) un clou [kloo]
nail clippers un coupe-ongles [koop-ONgl]
nail file une lime à ongles [leem ah ONgl]
nail polish du vernis à ongles [vairnee ah ONgl]
nail scissors des ciseaux à ongles [seezo ah ONgl]
naked nu [nɔo]
name un nom [nON]
  my name is... je m'appelle... [Juh ma-pel]
  what's your name? comment t'appelles-tu?
  [komON ta-pel-tɔo]
napkin une serviette [sairv-yet]

nappy une couche [koosh]
narrow étroit [ay-trwa]
national national [nass-yonal]
nationality la nationalité [nass-yonalee-tay]
natural naturel [natoo-rel]
near: is it near? est-ce que c'est près? [eskuh seh preh]
  near here près d'ici [...dee-see]
  do you go near...? est-ce que vous passez près de...? [eskuh voo pa-say...]
  where's the nearest...? où est le/la... le/la plus proche? [oo eh...luh/la ploo prosh]
nearly presque [presk]
neat *(drink)* sec
necessary nécessaire [naysess-sair]
  it's not necessary ce n'est pas nécessaire [suh neh pa...]
neck le cou [koo]
necklace le collier [kol-yay]
need: I need a... j'ai besoin d'un/une... [jay buh-zwan dan/doon]
needle une aiguille [ay-gwee]
neighbour le voisin [vwa-zan]
  (woman) la voisine [vwa-zeen]
neither: neither of them aucun/aucune des deux [o-kan/o-koon day duh]
  neither... nor... ni... ni... [nee...]
  neither am/do I moi non plus [mwa non ploo]
nephew: my nephew mon neveu [mon nuh-vuh]
nervous nerveux [nairvuh]
net *(sport, fishing)* le filet [feeleh]
nettoyage à sec dry cleaning
never jamais [ja-meh]
new nouveau/nouvelle [noovo/noovel]
  (not used) neuf [nurf]
news les nouvelles [noo-vel]
newsagent's un kiosque à journaux [kee-osk ah

Joorno]

newspaper un journal [Joor-nal]

do you have any English newspapers? est-ce que vous avez des journaux anglais? [eskuh voo zavay day Joorno ON-gleh]

New Year la nouvelle année [noo-vel anay]

Happy New Year bonne année [bon anay]

New Year's Eve la Saint-Sylvestre [SAN-seel-vestr]

> ✈ Usually an occasion for a big meal with friends (**le réveillon du Nouvel An**).

New Zealand la Nouvelle Zélande [noo-vel zay-lONd]

next prochain [proshAN]

at the next corner please au prochain croisement, s'il vous plaît [o proshAN krwaz-mON...]

see you next year à l'année prochaine! [ah lanay proshen]

next week/next Tuesday la semaine prochaine/mardi prochain

next to the hotel à côté de l'hôtel [ah ko-tay duh...]

next of kin le plus proche parent [plœ prosh parON]

nice *(good)* bon [bON]

(nice-looking) joli [Jolee]

(pleasant, kind) gentil [JON-tee]

niece: my niece ma nièce [...nee-yess]

night la nuit [nwee]

good night bonne nuit [bon...]

at night la nuit

night club une boîte de nuit [bwat duh nwee]

nightdress une chemise de nuit [shuh-meez duh nwee]

night porter le portier de nuit [port-yay duh nwee]

no non [NON]
  there's no water il n'y a pas d'eau [eel n-ya pa doh]
  I've no money je n'ai pas d'argent [Juh nay pa...]
nobody personne [pair-son]
  nobody saw it personne ne l'a vu [...nuh...]
noisy bruyant [brwee-yON]
  our room is too noisy notre chambre est trop bruyante [notr shONbr eh tro brwee-yONT]
none aucun/aucune [o-kAN/o-kOON]
  none of them aucun d'entre eux [...dONtr uh]
non-smoker: we're non-smokers nous ne fumons pas [noo nuh fOOmON pa]
nor: nor am/do I moi non plus [mwa NON plOO]
normal normal [nor-mal]
north le nord [nor]
Northern Ireland l'Irlande du Nord [eer-lOND dOO nor]
nose le nez [nay]
not pas [pa]
  not that one pas celui-là/celle-là [...suh-lwee-la/sel-la]
  not me pas moi [...mwa]

> To say 'not' with a verb you wrap **ne...pas** around the verb.
>   **I don't want to** je ne veux pas
>   **she isn't here** elle n'est pas là
>   **he didn't tell me** il ne me l'a pas dit

note *(money)* un billet (de banque) [bee-yeh duh bONK]
nothing rien [ree-yAN]
November novembre [no-vONbr]
now maintenant [mANt-nON]
nowhere nulle part [nOOl par]
nudist beach une plage réservée aux nudistes

[plahɹ rayzairvay o nɔɔdeest]
nuisance: it's a nuisance c'est ennuyeux [seh tON-nwee-yuh]
   this man's being a nuisance cet homme m'importune [set tom mANpor-tɔɔn]
numb engourdi [ONgoor-dee]
number *(figure)* le numéro [nɔɔmay-ro]
number plate la plaque d'immatriculation [plak deematree-kɔɔ-lass-yON]
nurse une infirmière [ANfeerm-yair]
   (male) un infirmier [ANfeerm-yay]
nursery slope une piste pour débutants [peest poor day-bɔɔtON]
nut la noix [nwa]
   (for bolt) un écrou [ay-kroo]

O [o]

oar une rame [rahm]
objets trouvés lost property
obligatory obligatoire [oblee-gatwahr]
obviously évidemment [ayvee-damON]
occasionally de temps en temps [duh tON zON...]
o'clock *go to* **time**
October octobre [ok-tobr]
octopus un poulpe [poolp]
odd *(number)* impair [AN-pair]
   (strange) bizarre
of de [duh]
   the name of the hotel le nom de l'hôtel

> **De**, used with **le**, becomes **du**. With the plural **les** it becomes **des**.
> **because of the price** à cause du prix
> **the children's room** la chambre des enfants

off: the milk is off le lait n'est plus bon [...neh

plœ bON]

it just came off ça s'est cassé tout seul [sa seh ka-say too surl]

10% off dix pour cent de réduction [dee poor sON duh raydœks-yON]

office un bureau [bœro]

officer (to policeman) monsieur l'agent [muhs-yuh la-JON]

(to woman) madame l'agent [ma-dam...]

often souvent [soovON]

how often? tous les combien? [too lay kONb-yAN]

(how many times?) combien de fois? [...duh fwa]

not often pas souvent [pa...]

how often do the buses go? il y a des bus tous les combien? [eelya day bœss too lay kONb-yAN]

> *YOU MAY THEN HEAR*
> toutes les dix minutes *every ten minutes*
> deux fois par jour *twice a day*

oil de l'huile [weel]

will you change the oil? est-ce que vous pouvez faire la vidange? [eskuh voo poovay fair la vee-dONJ]

ointment une pommade [pomad]

ok d'accord [da-kor]

it's ok (doesn't matter) ce n'est pas grave [suh neh pa grahv]

are you ok? ça va? [sa...]

that's ok by me ça me va [...muh...]

is this ok for the airport? (bus, train) c'est bien ça pour aller à l'aéroport? [seh b-yAN sa poor alay ah...]

more wine? – no, I'm ok thanks encore un peu de vin? – non, ça va merci [ON-kor AN puh duh vAN...]

old vieux/vieille [v-yuh/v-yay]

how old are you? quel âge avez-vous? [kel ahɹ avay-voo]

I am 28 j'ai vingt-huit ans [Jay...ON]

---

olive une olive [oleev]
olive oil de l'huile d'olive [weel doleev]
omelette une omelette [om-let]
on sur [sœr]
  I haven't got it on me je ne l'ai pas sur moi [Juh nuh lay pa sœr mwa]
  on Friday vendredi
  on television à la télévision [ah...]
once une fois [ɔɔn fwa]
  at once *(immediately)* tout de suite [toot sweet]
one un/une [ʌN/ɔɔn]
  (number) un
  the red one le/la rouge
onion un oignon [on-yON]
on-line: to pay on-line payer en ligne [pay-yay ON leen-yuh]
only seulement [surlmON]
  the only one le seul/la seule [surl]
open *(adjective)* ouvert [oovair]
  I can't open it je n'arrive pas à l'ouvrir [Juh nareev pa ah loovreer]
  when do you open? quand est-ce que vous ouvrez? [kONt eskuh voo zoo-vreh]
open ticket un billet open [bee-yeh...]
opera un opéra [opay-ra]
operation une opération [opay-rass-yON]
operator *(telephone)* l'opérateur [opay-ratur]
  (woman) l'opératrice [opay-ratreess]
opposite: opposite the hotel en face de l'hôtel [ON fass duh...]
optician's un opticien [opteess-yAN]
or ou [oo]
orange une orange [orONJ]

(colour) orange

orange juice un jus d'orange [Jœ doroNJ]

order: could we order now? est-ce qu'on peut *commander* maintenant? [eskON puh komoN-day mANt-noN]

   thank you, we've already ordered merci, nous avons déjà commandé [...noo zavoN day-Ja komoN-day]

other: the other one l'autre [ohtr]

   do you have any others? est-ce que vous en avez d'autres? [eskuh voo zoN navay...]

otherwise autrement [ohtruh-moN]

ought: I ought to go je *devrais* partir [Juh duh-vreh par-teer]

our notre [notr]

   (plural) nos [no]

ours le/la nôtre [luh/la nohtr]

   (plural) les nôtres

   it's ours c'est à nous [seh ta noo]

out: we're out of petrol nous n'avons plus d'essence [noo navoN plœ...]

   get out! dehors! [duh-or]

outboard un hors-bord [or-bor]

outdoors dehors [duh-or]

outside: can we sit outside? est-ce qu'on peut se mettre *dehors*? [eskoN puh suh metr duh-or]

ouvert open

over: over here ici [ee-see]

   over there là-bas [la-ba]

   over 40 plus de quarante [plœ duh...]

   it's all over *(finished)* c'est fini [seh fee-nee]

overcharge: you've overcharged me il y a une erreur dans la note [eelya œn air-rur doN la not]

overcooked trop cuit [tro kwee]

overexposed surexposé [sœrex-po-zay]

overnight *(stay, travel)* la nuit [nwee]

oversleep: I overslept j'ai dormi trop longtemps

[Jay dor-mee tro lon-ton]

overtake dépasser [daypasay]

owe: what do I owe you? combien est-ce que je vous *dois*? [konb-yan eskuh Juh voo dwa]

own: my own... mon/ma propre... [...propr]

    I'm on my own je suis seul [Juh swee surl]

owner le/la propriétaire [propree-yay-tair]

oxygen l'oxygène [oxee-Jen]

oysters des huîtres [weetr]

P [pay]

pack: I haven't packed yet je n'ai pas encore *fait mes bagages* [Juh nay pa zon-kor feh may bagahJ]

    can I have a packed lunch? est-ce que je peux avoir un pique-nique? [eskuh Juh puh avwahr an peek-neek]

package tour un voyage organisé [vwy-ahJ organee-zay]

page *(of book)* la page [pahJ]

    could you page him? est-ce que vous pouvez le faire appeler? [eskuh voo poovay luh fair aplay]

pain la douleur [doolur]

    I've got a pain in my... j'ai mal à... [Jay mal ah]

pain-killers des calmants [kal-mon]

painting *(picture)* un tableau [tablo]

Pakistan le Pakistan

pale pâle [pahl]

pancake une crêpe [krep]

panties un slip [sleep]

pants un pantalon [ponta-lon]

    (underpants) un slip [sleep]

paper du papier [pap-yay]

    (newspaper) un journal [Joor-nal]

parcel un colis [kolee]

pardon? *(didn't understand)* pardon? [par-don]

I beg your pardon excusez-moi [exkoo-zay mwa]

parents: my parents mes parents [may pa- RON]

Paris Paris [pa-ree]

park un parc [park]

where can I park my car? où est-ce que je peux *garer* ma voiture? [weskuh Juh puh garay ma vwatoor]

is it difficult to get parked? est-ce que c'est difficile de se garer? [eskuh seh deefee-seel duh suh garay]

parking ticket une contravention [kontravONss-yON]

part une partie [partee]

a (spare) part une pièce de rechange [pee-yess duh ruh-shONJ]

partner *(boyfriend)* le petit ami [puhtee ta-mee]
(girlfriend) la petite amie [puhteet a-mee]
(person you live with) le compagnon/la compagne [kONpan-yON/kONpan-yuh]

party *(group)* le groupe [groop]
(celebration) une fête [fet]
I'm with the...party je suis avec le groupe de... [Juh swee...]

pass *(in mountain)* le col
he's passed out il s'est évanoui [eel seh tayvan-wee]

passable *(road)* praticable [prat-ee-kahbl]

passage souterrain subway

passenger un passager [pasa-Jay]
(woman) une passagère [pasa-Jair]

passer-by un passant [pa-sON]
(woman) une passante [pa-sONt]

passport le passeport [paspor]

past: in the past autrefois [ohtr-fwa]
it's just past the traffic lights c'est juste *après* les feux [seh Joost apreh lay fuh]
go to **time**

path le sentier [sONt-yay]
patient: be patient soyez patient [swy-yay pas-yON]
pattern le dessin [dessAN]
pavement le trottoir [trotwahr]
pavement café un café en terrasse [...ON tair-rass]
pay payer [pay-yay]
   can I pay, please est-ce que je peux payer, s'il
   vous plaît? [eskuh Juh puh...]

> ✈ In bars and cafés you normally pay when
> you leave (with the exception of busy
> pavement cafés).

PCV: appel en PCV reverse charge call
peace la paix [peh]
peach une pêche [pesh]
péage toll
peanuts des cacahuètes [kaka-wet]
pear une poire [pwahr]
peas des petits pois [puhtee pwa]
pedal la pédale [pay-dahl]
pedestrian un piéton [pee-yay-tON]
pedestrian crossing un passage piétons [pa-sahJ
pee-yay-tON]

> ✈ Don't assume that the cars will stop or even
> slow down.

peg *(for washing)* une pince à linge [pANss ah lANJ]
   (for tent) un piquet de tente [peekeh duh tONt]
pen un stylo [steelo]
   have you got a pen? est-ce que vous avez un
   stylo? [eskuh voo zavay...]
pencil un crayon (de bois) [kreh-yON (duh bwa)]
penicillin la pénicilline [paynee-see-leen]
penknife un canif [kaneef]
pension (de famille) guesthouse
pensioner un retraité [ruhtreh-tay]
   (woman) une retraitée

people les gens [JON]
  how many people? combien de personnes?
[kONb-yAN duh pair-son]
people carrier un monospace [monospass]
pepper du poivre [pwahvr]
  a green/red pepper un poivron vert/rouge [AN
pwa-vrON vair/rooJ]
peppermint *(sweet)* un bonbon à la menthe [...
mONt]
per: per night/week/person par nuit/semaine/
personne
per cent pour cent [poor sON]
perfect parfait [par-feh]
  the perfect holiday des vacances idéales [va-
kONss eeday-ahl]
perfume le parfum [par-fAN]
perhaps peut-être [purt-etr]
périphérique ring road
period *(of time)* une période [payr-yod]
  (menstruation) les règles [regl]
perm une permanente [pairma-nONt]
permit un permis [pairmee]
person une personne [pair-son]
  in person en personne [ON...]
personal stereo un baladeur [baladur]
petrol de l'essence [ay-sONss]
petrol station une station-service [stass-yON sair-
veess]

✈ **Sans plomb** is unleaded. **Gasoil** is diesel.

pharmacy une pharmacie [farma-see]
phone le téléphone [taylay-fon]
  I'll phone you je vous/t'appelle *(polite/familiar)*
[Juh voo za-pel/ta-pel]
  I'll phone you back je vous/te rappelle *(polite/
familiar)* [...ra-pel]
  can you phone back in five minutes? pouvez-

vous rappeler dans cinq minutes? [poovay-voo
raplay...]

> **can I speak to...?** est-ce que je peux parler
> à...? [eskuh Juh puh parlay ah...]
> **could you get the number for me?** est-ce
> que vous pouvez m'appeler ce numéro?
> [eskuh voo poovay maplay suh nœmay-ro]

> *YOU MAY HEAR*
> qui est à l'appareil? *who's speaking?*
> c'est de la part de qui? *who's calling?*
> ne quittez pas *hold the line*
> bonjour, vous êtes sur la messagerie du...;
> veuillez laisser un message après le bip
> sonore *hello, you have reached the voicemail
> of...; please leave a message after the tone*

phonebox une cabine téléphonique [kabeen
taylay-foneek]

> ✈ Nearly all of them take phonecards or credit
> cards only.

phonecall un coup de téléphone [koo duh taylay-
fon]
can I make a phonecall? est-ce que je peux
téléphoner? [eskuh Juh puh taylay-fonay]
phonecard une télécarte [taylay-kart]

> ✈ You can buy one from a newsagent,
> **bureau de tabac** or post office.

photograph une photo
would you take a photograph of us/me?
est-ce que vous pouvez nous/me prendre en
photo? [eskuh voo poovay noo/muh proNdr oN...]
piano un piano
pickpocket un pickpocket
picture *(painting)* le tableau

piece un morceau [morso]
  a piece of... un morceau de...
piétons, attention, traversez en 2 temps
pedestrians, be careful, cross in 2 stages
pig un cochon [koshON]
pigeon un pigeon [pee-JON]
pile-up un carambolage [karONbolahJ]
pill une pilule [pee-lool]
  are you on the pill? est-ce que vous prenez la
  pilule? [eskuh voo pruh-nay la...]
pillow un oreiller [oray-yay]
pin une épingle [ay-pANgl]
pineapple un ananas [ana-nass]
pink rose [roz]
pint

> ✈ 1 pint = 0.57 litres

pipe *(to smoke)* une pipe [peep]
  (for water) le tuyau [twee-yo]
pity: it's a pity c'est dommage [seh domahJ]
place un endroit [ON-drwa]
  is this place taken? est-ce que cette place est
  prise? [eskuh set plass eh preez]
  do you know any good places to go? est-ce
  que vous connaissez des endroits intéressants?
  [eskuh voo konessay dayz...ANtay-ressON]
  at my place chez moi [shay mwa]
  at your place chez vous/toi *(polite/familiar)*
  [...voo/twa]
  to your place chez vous/toi
places assises seated accommodation
places debout standing room
plain simple [sANpl]
  (not patterned) uni [oo-nee]
  a plain omelette une omelette nature [...na-
  toor]
plane l'avion [av-yON]

on the plane dans l'avion [doN...]
plant une plante [plONt]
plaster *(cast)* un plâtre [plahtr]
  (sticking) un pansement [poNss-moN]
plastic en plastique [ON plasteek]
plastic bag un sac plastique [...plasteek]
plate une assiette [ass-yet]
platform *(station)* le quai [keh]
  which platform? quel quai? [kel...]
play jouer [Joo-ay]
pleasant agréable [agray-ahbl]
please: could you please...? s'il vous plaît, est-
  ce que vous pouvez...? [seel voo pleh eskuh voo
  poovay]
  (yes) please oui, s'il vous plaît [wee...]
pleasure le plaisir [plezeer]
  it's a pleasure de rien [duh ree-yAN]
plenty: plenty of... beaucoup de... [bo-koo duh]
  thank you, that's plenty merci, ça suffit [...sa
  soo-fee]
pliers des tenailles [tuh-nI]
plug *(electrical)* la prise [preez]
  (for car) la bougie [boo-Jee]
  (for sink) la bonde [boNd]

➔ Two-pin plugs are the norm.

plum une prune [proon]
plumber un plombier [ploNb-yay]
plus plus [ploos]
pm: 1 pm une heure *de l'après-midi* [oon ur duh
  lapreh-mee-dee]
  7 pm sept heures *du soir* [set ur doo swahr]

➔ The 24-hour system is commonly used in
  spoken French. 1 pm is **treize heures**; 7
  pm is **dix-neuf heures**.

pocket la poche [posh]

poids lourds heavy goods vehicles

point: could you point to it? est-ce que vous pouvez me l'*indiquer*? [eskuh voo poovay muh lANdee-kay]

4 point 6 4 virgule 6 [...veer-gool...]

police la police [poleess]

get the police appelez la police [aplay...]

> ✈ Dial 17. Dial 112 from a mobile for any emergency.

policeman un agent de police [ah-JON duh poleess]

police station le commissariat [komee-sahr-ya]

policewoman une femme policier [fam poleesee-yay]

polish du cirage [seerahJ]

can you polish my shoes? est-ce que vous pouvez faire cirer mes chaussures? [eskuh voo poovay fair seeray may sho-soor]

polite poli [polee]

polluted pollué [poloo-ay]

pool *(swimming)* la piscine [pee-seen]

poor: I'm very poor je suis très pauvre [Juh swee treh pohvr]

poor quality de mauvaise qualité [duh mo-vez kaleetay]

pork du porc [por]

port un port [por]

(drink) du porto

to port *(not starboard)* à bâbord [ah ba-bor]

porter *(in hotel)* le portier [port-yay]

portrait un portrait [por-treh]

Portugal le Portugal [portoogal]

posh chic [sheek]

possible possible [posseebl]

could you possibly...? est-ce que vous pourriez...? [eskuh voo poor-yay]

post (mail) le courrier [koor-yay]
postbox une boîte aux lettres [bwat o letr]
postcard une carte postale [kart poss-tahl]
poste restante la poste restante [posst restONT]
post office la poste [posst]
potatoes des pommes de terre [pom duh tair]
pound (weight, money) une livre [leevr]

✈ pounds/11 x 5 = kilos

pounds	1	3	5	6	7	8	9
kilos	0.45	1.4	2.3	2.7	3.2	3.6	4.1

poussez push
pour: it's pouring il pleut à verse [eel pluh ah vairss]
power cut une panne d'électricité [pan daylek-tree-see-tay]
power point une prise de courant [preez duh koo-rON]
prawns des crevettes [kruh-vet]
prefer: I prefer this one je préfère celui-ci/celle-ci [Juh pray-fair...]
   I'd prefer to... je préférerais... [Juh pray-fair-uh-reh]
   I'd prefer a... je préférerais un/une...
pregnant enceinte [ON-sANt]
prescription une ordonnance [ordonONss]
present: at present à présent [ah pray-zON]
   here's a present for you voilà un cadeau pour vous [vwahla AN ka-doh poor voo]
president (of country) le président [prayzee-dON]
   (woman) la présidente [prayzee-dONt]
press: could you press these? est-ce que vous pouvez *repasser* ces vêtements? [eskuh voo poovay ruhpasay say vet-mON]
presse newsagent
pressing dry cleaner's
prêt-à-porter ready-to-wear

pretty joli [Jolee]
  pretty good pas mal [pa...]
  pretty expensive assez cher [assay...]
price le prix [pree]
prière de... please...
prière de ne pas... please do not...
priest un prêtre [pretr]
primeurs early produce
priorité (à droite) vehicles coming from the
  right have priority
prison la prison [pree-ZON]
private privé [preevay]
probably probablement [pro-ba-bluh-mON]
problem un problème [prob-lem]
  no problem! pas de problème! [pa duh...]
product un produit [prodwee]
profit le bénéfice [baynay-feess]
promise: do you promise? vous le promettez?
  [voo luh prometay]
  I promise je vous/te le promets *(polite/familiar)*
  [Juh voo/tuh luh promeh]
pronounce: how do you pronounce this?
  comment est-ce que ça se prononce? [komON
  eskuh sa suh pronONss]
propeller une hélice [ay-leess]
properly correctement [korek-tuh-mON]
propriété privée private, no trespassing
prostitute une prostituée [prosteetoo-ay]
protect protéger [protay-Jay]
protection factor l'indice de protection [ANdeess
  duh proteks-yON]
Protestant protestant [protestON]
proud fier [fee-yair]
public: the public le public [poobleek]
public convenience des toilettes publiques [twa-
  let poobleek]

➤ You can use the toilet in cafés or bars but you're supposed to buy something too. Or pay to go into one of the slightly futuristic toilet cabins on the street.

public holiday un jour férié [Joor fayr-yay]

➤ Jan 1st, **le premier de l'An**, New Year's Day
Easter Monday, **le lundi de Pâques**
May 1st, **le premier mai**, **la fête du travail**, May Day
Ascension Day, **le jeudi de l'Ascension**
Whit Sunday and Whit Monday **la Pentecôte**
July 14th, **le quatorze juillet**, Bastille Day
Aug 15th, **l'Assomption**, **le quinze août**, Assumption
Nov 1st, **la Toussaint**, All Saints' Day
Nov 11th, **le onze novembre**, Remembrance Day
Dec 25th, **Noël**, Christmas Day

pudding un pudding
(dessert) un dessert [day-sair]
pull *(verb)* tirer [tee-ray]
he pulled out in front of me il a déboîté juste devant moi [eel ah daybwatay Jɔɔst duh-VON mwa]
pump la pompe [PONp]
puncture une crevaison [kruh-vɛzON]
pure pur [pɔɔr]
purple violet [vee-yoleh]
purse le porte-monnaie [port-moneh]
push *(verb)* pousser [poo-say]
pushchair une poussette [poo-set]
put: where can I put...? où est-ce que je peux *mettre*...? [weskuh Juh puh metr]
pyjamas un pyjama [peeJa-ma]

Q [koo]

quai *(at station)* platform
quality la qualité [kaleetay]
quarantine la quarantaine [karON-ten]
quarter un quart [kar]
  a quarter of an hour un quart d'heure [kar dur]
  go to **time**
quay le quai [keh]
question une question [kest-yON]

> One common way of asking a question
> is to put **est-ce que** in front of the
> statement.
>   **it's finished** c'est fini
>   **is it finished?** est-ce que c'est fini? [eskuh
>   seh...]

queue une file d'attente [feel datONt]
quick rapide [ra-peed]
  that was quick c'était rapide [say-teh...]
quiet tranquille [trON-keel]
  be quiet! taisez-vous! [tezzay-voo]
quite très [treh]
  (fairly) assez [assay]
  quite a lot pas mal [pa...]

R [air]

radiator le radiateur [rad-yatur]
radio la radio [rad-yo]
rail: by rail en train [ON trAN]
rain la pluie [plwee]
  it's raining il pleut [eel pluh]
raincoat un imperméable [ANpair-may-ahbl]
ralentir slow down
ralentissement slow-moving traffic

rally *(cars)* le rallye [ra-lee]
rape un viol [vee-ol]
rappel reminder
rare rare [rar]
  (steak) saignant [sen-yON]
raspberry la framboise [frON-bwaz]
rat un rat [ra]
rather: I'd rather have a... j'aimerais mieux avoir un/une... [Jemreh m-yuh avwahr AN/oon]
  I'd rather sit here je préférerais m'asseoir ici [pray-fair-ray...]
  I'd rather not j'aime mieux pas [Jem m-yuh pa]
  it's rather hot il fait *plutôt* chaud [eel feh plooto sho]
raw cru [kroo]
razor un rasoir [raz-wahr]
read: something to read quelque chose à *lire* [kelkuh shohz ah leer]
ready: when will it be ready? ce sera *prêt* quand? [suh suh-ra preh kON]
  I'm not ready yet je ne suis pas encore prêt/ prête [Juh nuh swee pa zON-kor preh/pret]
real véritable [vayree-tahbl]
really vraiment [vreh-mON]
rear-view mirror le rétroviseur [raytro-vee-zur]
reasonable raisonnable [reh-zonahbl]
receipt un reçu [ruh-soo]
  (in shop) un ticket [teekeh]
recently récemment [raysa-mON]
reception la réception [rayseps-yON]
  in reception à la réception
receptionist le/la réceptionniste [rayseps-yoneest]
recipe une recette [ruh-set]
recommend: can you recommend...? est-ce que vous pouvez recommander...? [eskuh voo poovay ruh-komON-day]
red rouge [rooJ]

reduction *(in price)* une réduction [raydooks-yON]

red wine un vin rouge [VAN...]

refuse: I refuse je refúse [Juh ruh-fooz]

region la région [rayJ-yON]

registered: I want to send this registered
j'aimerais envoyer ça *en recommandé* [Jemreh
ONvwy-yay sa ON ruh-komON-day]

relais routier

> ✈ Inexpensive restaurants catering primarily
> for transport drivers; look for the red and
> blue circular sign.

relax: I just want to relax je veux simplement
me détendre [Juh vuh sANpluh-mON muh day-
tONdr]

relax! détendez-vous! [daytONday-voo]

remember: don't you remember? vous ne vous
souvenez pas? [voo nuh voo soo-vuhnay pa]

I don't remember je ne me souviens pas [Juh
nuh muh soov-yAN pa]

renseignements enquiries

rent: can I rent a car/bicycle? est-ce que je
peux *louer* une voiture/un vélo? [eskuh Juh puh
loo-ay oon vwatoor/AN vaylo]

> *YOU MAY HEAR*
> quel modèle? *what type?*
> pour combien de jours? *for how many
> days?*
> ramenez-la avant... *bring it back before...*
> kilométrage illimité *unlimited mileage*

---

rental car une voiture de location [vwatoor duh
lokass-yON]

rep le représentant [ruhpray-zONtON]
(woman) la représentante [ruhpray-zONtONt]
(activities organizer) l'animateur [aneematur]
(woman) l'animatrice [aneematreess]

repair: can you repair it? est-ce que vous pouvez le/la *réparer*? [eskuh voo poovay luh/la raypa-ray]

repeat: could you repeat that? est-ce que vous pouvez *répéter*? [eskuh voo poovay raypay-tay]

reputation la réputation [raypootass-yON]

R.E.R [air-uh-air] fast commuter train in the Greater Paris area

rescue *(verb)* sauver [so-vay]

reservation une réservation [rayzair-vass yON]
  I want to make a reservation for... j'aimerais réserver... [Jemreh rayzair-vay]

reserve: can I reserve a seat? est-ce que je peux réserver une place? [eskuh Juh puh rayzair-vay oon plass]

> *YOU MAY THEN HEAR*
> pour quelle heure? *for what time?*
> à quel nom? *and your name is?*

responsible responsable [respON-sahbl]

rest: I've come here for a rest je suis venu ici pour *me reposer* [...muh ruhpo-zay]
  you keep the rest gardez la monnaie [garday la moneh]

restaurant un restaurant [resto-rON]

restaurant car le wagon-restaurant [vagON-resto-rON]

retired à la retraite [ah la ruh-tret]

return: a return to... un aller-retour pour... [...alay ruh-toor poor]

reverse charge call un appel en PCV [...ON pay-say-vay]

reverse gear la marche arrière [marsh aree-yair]

rez-de-chaussée ground floor

rheumatism des rhumatismes [roomateess-muh]

rib une côte [koht]

rice du riz [ree]
rich riche [reesh]
ridiculous ridicule [reedee-kool]
right: that's right c'est vrai [seh vreh]
  you're right vous avez raison [voo zavay reh-zON]
    right! *(understood)* d'accord! [da-kor]
    on the right à droite [ah drwat]
righthand drive avec le volant à droite [...volON ah drwat]
ring *(on finger)* une bague [bag]
ripe mûr [moor]
rip-off: it's a rip-off c'est de l'arnaque [seh duh larnak]
river une rivière [reev-yair]
  (big) un fleuve [flurv]
road une route [root]
  which is the road to...? quelle est la route pour...? [kel eh...]
road map une carte routière [kart root-yair]
rob: I've been robbed on m'a *dévalisé* [ON ma dayvalee-zay]
rock un rocher [roshay]
  whisky on the rocks whisky avec de la glace [...ah-vek duh la glass]
roll *(bread)* un petit pain [puhtee pAN]
romantic romantique [romON-teek]
roof le toit [twa]
roof box le coffre de toit [kofr duh twa]
roof rack la galerie [gal-ree]
room *(in hotel)* la chambre [shONbr]
  (in house) la pièce [p-yess]
    have you got a single/double room?
    est-ce que vous avez une chambre pour une personne/deux personnes? [eskuh voo zavay...poor oon pair-son/duh pair-son]

for one night pour une nuit [poor ɔn nwee]
for three nights pour trois nuits [...trwa nwee]

YOU MAY THEN HEAR
pour combien de nuits? *for how many nights?*
avec douche? *with shower?*
avec salle de bains? *with bath?*
je suis désolé mais c'est complet *sorry, but we're full*

---

room service le service en chambre [sair-veess ON shoNbr]
rope une corde [kord]
rose une rose [roz]
rough *(sea)* agité [aJeetay]
roughly *(approx)* à peu près [ah puh preh]
round *(circular)* rond [roN]
  it's my round c'est ma tournée [seh ma toornay]
roundabout *(on road)* le rond-point [roN-pwaN]

✈ Priority to the cars already on the round-about. Remember they'll be coming from the left. Don't forget to take it anticlockwise.

route un itinéraire [eetee-nay-rair]
  which is the prettiest/fastest route? quel est l'itinéraire le plus agréable/rapide? [kel eh...luh ploo zagray-ahbl/ra-peed]
rowing boat une barque [bark]
rubber *(material)* du caoutchouc [ka-oo-tchoo]
  (eraser) une gomme [gom]
rubber band un élastique [aylasteek]
rubbish *(waste)* les ordures [or-door]
  (poor quality goods) de la camelote [kamlot]

rubbish! n'importe quoi! [nANport kwa]
rucksack le sac à dos [sak ah doh]
rudder le gouvernail [goovairnɪ]
rude impoli [ANpolee]
ruin la ruine [roo-een]
rum du rhum [rom]
  a rum and coke un rhum coca
run (person) courir [koo-reer]
  hurry, run! vite, dépêchez-vous! [veet daypeshay-voo]
  I've run out of petrol/money je n'ai plus d'essence/d'argent [Juh nay ploo day-sONss/dar-JON]

S [ess]

sables mouvants quicksand
sad triste [treest]
safe (not dangerous) sans danger [sON dON-Jay]
  (not in danger) en sécurité [ON saykoo-ree-tay]
  will it be safe here? est-ce que ça ne risque rien ici? [eskuh sa nuh reesk ree-yAN ee-see]
  is it safe to swim here? est-ce qu'on peut se baigner sans danger ici? [eskON puh suh ben-yay sON dON-Jay...]
safety la sécurité [saykoo-ree-tay]
safety pin une épingle de sûreté [ay-pANgl duh soor-tay]
sail: can we go sailing? est-ce qu'on peut *faire de la voile*? [eskON puh fair duh la vwahl]
sailboard une planche à voile [plONsh ah vwahl]
sailboarding: to go sailboarding faire de la planche à voile [fair duh la plONsh ah vwahl]
sailor un marin [ma-rAN]
  he's a keen sailor c'est un passionné de voile [pass-yonay duh vwahl]
salad une salade [sa-lad]

salami le salami
sale: is it for sale? c'est à vendre? [seh ta vONdr]
salle à manger dining room
salle d'attente waiting room
salmon le saumon [so-mON]
salt le sel
same le/la même [mem]
   the same again, please la même chose, s'il
   vous plaît [la mem shohz...]
   it's all the same to me ça m'est égal [sa met
   ay-gal]
SAMU emergency ambulance, paramedics
sand le sable [sahbl]
sandals les sandales [sON-dahl]
sandwich un sandwich [sONd-weetch]
   a ham/cheese sandwich un sandwich au
   jambon/fromage [...oh JON-bON/fromahJ]

  ✈ Try the traditional **jambon beurre**, half a
    baguette with butter and ham.

sanitary towels des serviettes hygiéniques [sairv-
  yet eeJ-yay-neek]
sans issue no through road
satisfactory satisfaisant [sateess-fuh-zON]
Saturday samedi [sam-dee]
sauce la sauce [sohss]
saucepan une casserole [kass-rohl]
saucer une soucoupe [soo-koop]
sauna un sauna [so-na]
sausage une saucisse [so-seess]
  (cold) un saucisson [sosee-sON]
say dire [deer]
   how do you say...in French? comment est-ce
   qu'on dit en français...? [komON eskON dee ON
   frON-seh]
   what did he say? qu'est-ce qu'il a dit? [keskeel
   ah dee]

scarf un foulard [foo-lar]
  (woolly) une écharpe [aysharp]
scenery le paysage [payee-zahJ]
schedule l'horaire [o-rair]
  (programme) un programme
  on schedule à l'heure [ah lur]
  behind schedule en retard [ON ruh-tar]
scheduled flight un vol régulier [vol raygool-yay]
school l'école [aykol]
scissors: a pair of scissors une paire de ciseaux
  [pair duh seezo]
scooter un scooter [skootur]
Scotland l'Écosse [aykoss]
Scottish écossais/écossaise [aykosseh/aykossez]
scream *(verb)* crier [kree-yay]
  (noun) un cri [kree]
screw la vis [veess]
screwdriver un tournevis [toornuh-veess]
sea la mer [mair]
  by the sea au bord de la mer [o bor duh...]
seafood des fruits de mer [frweed mair]
search *(verb)* chercher [shair-shay]
search party une expédition de secours [expay-
  deess-yON duh suh-koor]
seasick: I get seasick j'ai le mal de mer [Jay luh
  mal duh mair]
seaside le bord de la mer [bor duh la mair]
  let's go to the seaside allons au bord de la mer
  [alON o...]
season la saison [sezON]
  in the high/low season en haute/basse saison
  [ON oht/bas...]
seasoning l'assaisonnement [asezon-mON]
seat un siège [see-eJ]
  (in train etc) une place [plass]
  is this somebody's seat? est-ce que cette place
  est occupée? [eskuh set plass eh tokoopay]

seat belt la ceinture de sécurité [sAN-toor duh saykoo-ree-tay]

✈ Compulsory front and back.

sea-urchin un oursin [oorsAN]
seaweed des algues [alg]
second *(adjective)* deuxième [durz-yem]
  (of time) une seconde [suh-gOND]
  the second of... *(date)* le deux... [duh]
secondhand d'occasion [dokaz-yON]
see voir [vwahr]
  have you seen...? est-ce que vous avez vu...? [eskuh voo zavay voo]
  can I see the room? est-ce que je peux voir la chambre? [eskuh Juh puh vwahr...]
  see you! au revoir! [o ruh-vwahr]
  see you tonight à ce soir [ah suh swahr]
  oh, I see ah, je vois [... Juh vwa]
self-catering apartment un appartement (de vacances) [apartmON (duh vakONss)]
self-service le self-service [...sair-veess]
sell vendre [vONdɪ]
send envoyer [ONvwy-yay]
  I want to send this to England j'aimerais envoyer ceci en Angleterre [jemreh...suhsee ON ONgluh-tair]
sensitive sensible [sON-seebl]
sens unique one way
separate *(adjective)* séparé [sayparay]
  I'm separated je suis séparé(e) [Juh swee sayparay]
separately: can we pay separately? est-ce qu'on peut payer séparément [eskON puh pay-yay sayparaymON]
September septembre [septONbr]
serious sérieux [say-ree-yuh]
  is it serious, doctor? est-ce que c'est grave,

docteur? [eskuh seh grahv...]
I'm serious je ne plaisante pas [Juh nuh plezONt pa]

serrez à droite keep to the right

service: is service included? est-ce que le service est compris? [eskuh luh sairveess eh kONpree]

service station une station-service [stass-YON-sairveess]

services *(on motorway)* une aire de services [air duh sairveess]

serviette une serviette [sairv-yet]

several plusieurs [plœz-yur]

sex le sexe [sex]

sexy sexy

shade: in the shade à l'ombre [ah lONbr]

shake secouer [suhkoo-ay]
to shake hands se serrer la main [suh suhray la mAN]

✈ Common on meeting or leaving somebody.

shallow peu profond [puh profON]

shame: what a shame! quel dommage! [kel domahJ]

shampoo un shampooing [shON-pwAN]

shandy une bière panachée [bee-yair panashay]

share *(room, table)* partager [partaJay]

shark un requin [ruh-kAN]

sharp coupant [koopON]
(taste) âpre [ahpr]
(pain) violent [veeolON]

shave se raser [suh razay]

shaver un rasoir [raz-wahr]

shaving foam de la mousse à raser [...ah razay]

shaving point une prise pour rasoir [preez poor raz-wahr]

she elle [el]

sheet un drap [dra]

shelf l'étagère [ayta-Jair]
shell *(sea-)* un coquillage [kokee-yahJ]
shellfish des coquillages [kokee-yahJ]
shelter un abri [ah-bree]
  can we shelter here? est-ce que nous pouvons nous abriter ici? [eskuh noo poovoN noo zah-bree-tay ee-see]
sherry un Xérès [gzay-ress]
ship le bateau [bato]
shirt une chemise [shuh-meez]
shit! merde! [maird]
shock un choc [shok]
  I got an electric shock from the... j'ai reçu une décharge électrique de... [Jay ruh-soo oon day-shahrJ aylek-treek duh]
shock-absorber l'amortisseur [amortee-sur]
shoelaces des lacets [lasseh]
shoes les chaussures [sho-soor]

✈ men:			40	41	42	43	44	45
women:	36	37	38	39	40	41		
UK:	3	4	5	6	7	8	9	10	11

shop le magasin [maga-zaN]
  I've some shopping to do j'ai des courses à faire [Jay day koorss ah fair]

> ✈ Small shops may close between 12 and 2 pm, especially in small towns. Usual opening hours: 9 am-7 pm. Bakers are open very early in the morning (usually 7 am). On Sunday mornings some small supermarkets will be open.

shop assistant un vendeur [voNdur]
  (female) une vendeuse [voNdurz]
short court [koor]
  (person) petit [puhtee]
short cut un raccourci [rakoor-see]

shorts le short [short]

shoulder l'épaule [ay-pohl]

shout crier [kree-yay]

show: please show me montrez-moi, s'il vous plaît [moN-tray mwa...]

shower: with shower avec douche [...doosh]

shrimps des crevettes grises [kruh-vet greez]

shut fermer [fairmay]

  they're shut c'est fermé [seh fairmay]

  when do you shut? vous fermez à quelle heure? [voo fairmay ah kel ur]

  shut up! taisez-vous! [tezzay-voo]

  (familiar) tais-toi [teh-twa]

shy timide [tee-meed]

sick malade [ma-lad]

  I feel sick je ne me sens pas bien [Juh nuh muh soN pa b-yaN]

  he's been sick il a vomi [eel ah vomee]

side le côté [ko-tay]

  by the side of the road au bord de la route [o bor duh la root]

side street une rue transversale [roo troNss-vairsal]

sight: the sights of... les choses à voir à... [lay shohz ah vwahr ah]

sightseeing tour une visite guidée [veezeet ghee-day]

sign *(notice)* l'écriteau [aykreeto]

  (road) un panneau [pano]

signal: he didn't signal il n'a pas mis son clignotant [eel na pa mee soN kleen-yotoN]

signature la signature [seen-yatoor]

silence le silence [seeloNss]

silencer le silencieux [seeloNss-yuh]

silk la soie [swa]

silly stupide [stoopeed]

silver l'argent [arJoN]

similar semblable [soN-blahbl]

simple simple [sANpl]

since: since last week depuis la semaine dernière [duh-pwee...]

  since we arrived depuis notre arrivée

  (because) puisque [pweeskuh]

sincere sincère [sANsair]

sing chanter [shONtay]

single: I'm single je suis célibataire [Juh swee saylee-ba-tair]

  a single to... un aller simple pour... [alay sANpl poor...]

single room une chambre pour une personne [shONbr poor ∞n pair-son]

sister: my sister ma sœur [...sur]

sit: can I sit here? est-ce que je peux *m'asseoir* ici? [eskuh Juh puh maswahr...]

size la taille [tɪ]

  (of shoes) la pointure [pwAN-t∞r]

skates des patins [pa-tAN]

ski le ski [skee]

  (verb) faire du ski [fair d∞...]

ski boots des chaussures de ski [sho-s∞r duh skee]

skid déraper [dayrapay]

skiing le ski [skee]

ski lift le remonte-pente [ruh-mONt-pONt]

skin la peau [po]

skin-diving la plongée sous-marine [plON-Jay soo-mareen]

ski pants le fuseau [f∞zo]

ski pole le bâton de skis [bah-tON duh skee]

skirt une jupe [J∞p]

ski slope une piste [peest]

ski wax le fart [far]

sky le ciel [see-yel]

sledge la luge [l∞J]

sleep: I can't sleep je ne peux pas dormir [...dor-meer]

sleeper *(rail)* le wagon-lit [va-gON-lee]
sleeping bag un sac de couchage [sak duh koo-shahJ]
sleeping pill un somnifère [somnee-fair]
sleeve la manche [mONsh]
slide *(photo)* une diapositive [dee-apozee-teev]
slow lent [lON]
   could you speak a little slower? est-ce que
   vous pouvez parler un peu plus lentement?
   [eskuh voo poovay parlay AN puh plœ lONT-mON]
slowly lentement [lONt-mON]
small petit [puhtee]
   smaller notes des petites coupures [day puhteet
   koopœr]
small change de la petite monnaie [puhteet
   moneh]
smell: there's a funny smell il y a une *odeur*
   bizarre [eelya œn o-dur...]
   it smells ça sent mauvais [sa sON mo-veh]
smile *(verb)* sourire [sooreer]
smoke la fumée [fœmay]
   do you smoke? est-ce que vous fumez? [eskuh
   voo fœmay]
   can I smoke? est-ce que je peux fumer? [eskuh
   Juh puh...]

  ✈ Public places are non-smoking.

snack un 'snack'
   can we just have a snack? est-ce que nous
   pouvons juste avoir un snack? [eskuh noo
   poovON Joost avwahr AN...]
snake un serpent [sair-pON]
S.N.C.F. French Railways
snorkel un tuba [tœba]
snow la neige [neJ]
   it's snowing il neige
so si

it's so hot today il fait *tellement* chaud aujourd'hui [eel feh telmON sho oJoordwee]
not so much pas autant [pa o-tON]
so am/do I moi aussi [mwa o-see]
soap le savon [sa-VON]
soap powder de la lessive en poudre [lesseev ON poodr]
sober sobre [sobr]
socks les chaussettes [sho-set]
soda (water) de l'eau de seltz [o...]
soft drink une boisson sans alcool [bwa-sON sON zal-kol]
soldes sale
sole la semelle [suh-mel]
some: some bread du pain [d∞...]
  some beer de la bière [duh la...]
  some crisps des chips [day...]
  can I have some? est-ce que je peux *en* avoir? [eskuh Juh puh ON navwahr]
somebody quelqu'un [kelkAN]
something quelque chose [kelkuh shohz]
sometimes quelquefois [kelkuh fwa]
somewhere quelque part [kelkuh par]
son: my son mon fils [mON feess]
song une chanson [shON-sON]
sonnez please ring
soon bientôt [b-yANto]
  as soon as possible dès que possible [deh kuh posseebl]
  sooner plus tôt [pl∞ toh]
sore: it's sore ça fait mal [sa feh mal]
sore throat mal à la gorge [mal ah la gorJ]
sorry: (I'm) sorry excusez-moi [exk∞-zay mwa]
  sorry? pardon? [par-dON]
sort: this sort cette sorte [set sort]
  what sort of...? quelle sorte de....? [kel...duh]
  will you sort it out? est-ce que vous pouvez

arranger ça? [eskuh voo poovay ah-roN-Jay sa]

sortie exit, way out

sortie de camions lorries crossing

sortie de secours emergency exit

so-so comme ci, comme ça [komsee-komsa]

soup la soupe [soop]

sour aigre [egr]

sous-sol basement

south le sud [sood]

South Africa l'Afrique du Sud [ah-freek doo sood]

souvenir un souvenir [soov-neer]

spade une pelle [pel]

Spain l'Espagne [espan-yuh]

Spanish espagnol [espan-yol]

spanner une clé anglaise [klay oN-glez]

spare part une pièce de rechange [pee-yess duh ruh-shoNJ]

spare wheel la roue de secours [roo duh suh-koor]

spark plug une bougie [boo-Jee]

speak parler [parlay]

  do you speak English? est-ce que vous parlez anglais? [eskuh voo parlay oN-gleh]

  I don't speak French je ne parle pas français [Juh nuh parl pa froN-seh]

special spécial [spayss-yal]

specialist un/une spécialiste [spayss-yaleest]

spectacles des lunettes [loo-net]

speed la vitesse [veetess]

  he was speeding il allait trop vite [eel alay tro veet]

speed limit la limitation de vitesse [leemee-tass-yoN...]

✈ In towns 50 kmh (31 mph); out of town 90 kmh (56 mph); on dual carriageways 110 kmh (69 mph); on M-ways 130 kmh (81 mph).

speedometer le compteur de vitesse [kON-tur...]

spend *(money)* dépenser [day-pON-say]

spice une épice [aypeess]

  is it spicy? est-ce que c'est très épicé? [eskuh seh treh zaypee-say]

spider une araignée [arayn-yay]

spoon une cuillère [kwee-yair]

sprain: I've sprained my... je me suis foulé le/la... [Juh muh swee foo-lay...]

spring *(of car, seat)* un ressort [ruh-sor]

  (season) le printemps [prAN-tON]

square *(in town)* la place [plass]

  two square metres deux mètres carrés [...metr karay]

stairs les escaliers [eskal-yay]

stalls l'orchestre [or-kestr]

stamp un timbre [tANbr]

  two stamps for England deux timbres pour l'Angleterre

> ✈ Buy stamps at post offices or at a **bureau de tabac**. Look for the sign: **tabac** (sometimes a section of a café). First class are red (**tarif urgent**); second class green (**tarif lent**).

stand *(at fair)* un stand [stONd]

stand-by: to fly stand-by voyager en 'stand-by' [vwy-ahJay ON...]

star l'étoile [ay-twal]

starboard tribord [tree-bor]

start: when does it start? ça commence quand? [sa komONss kON]

  my car won't start ma voiture ne démarre pas [ma vwatœr nuh day-mar pa]

starter *(of car)* le démarreur [dayma-rur]

  (food) une entrée [ON-tray]

starving: I'm starving je meurs de faim [Juh mur

duh fAN]

station la gare [gar]

   (underground) la station de métro [stass-yON...]

stationnement parking

stationnement gênant no parking

stationnement payant pay-and-display

statue une statue [statoo]

stay le séjour [say-Joor]

   we enjoyed our stay nous avons passé un très bon séjour [noo zavON pa-say AN treh bON...]

   stay there restez là [restay la]

   I'm staying at... je suis descendu à... [Juh swee day-sONdoo ah]

steak un steak [stek]

YOU MAY HEAR
quelle cuisson? *how would you like it done?*
à point *medium*
bien cuit *well done*
saignant *rare*

✈ Rare will be very rare.

steal: my wallet's been stolen on m'a *volé* mon portefeuille [ON ma volay...]

steep raide [red]

steering la direction [deereks-yON]

steering wheel le volant [volON]

step *(of stairs)* la marche [marsh]

sterling livres sterling [leevr stair-ling]

stewardess une hôtesse [o-tess]

sticking plaster un pansement [pONss-mON]

sticky collant [kol-ON]

stiff raide [red]

still: keep still ne bougez pas [nuh booJay pa]

   I'm still here je suis *encore* là [Juh swee zON-kor la]

   I'm still waiting j'attends *toujours* [JatON

tooJoor]

sting: I've been stung j'ai été piqué [Jay ay-tay pee-kay]

stink la puanteur [pœ-ONtur]

stink: it stinks ça pue [sa pœ]

stomach l'estomac [estoma]

  have you got something for an upset stomach? est-ce que vous avez quelque chose pour les maux de ventre? [eskuh voo zavay kelkuh shohz poor lay mo duh vONtr]

stomach-ache: I have a stomach-ache j'ai mal au ventre [Jay mal o vONtr]

stone une pierre [p-yair]

  ✈ 1 stone = 6.35 kilos

stop *(for buses)* un arrêt [areh]

  stop! arrêtez! [aretay]

  do you stop near...? est-ce que vous vous arrêtez près de...? [eskuh voo voo zaretay preh duh]

  could you stop here? est-ce que vous pouvez vous arrêter ici? [...ee-see]

stop-over une escale [eskal]

storm une tempête [toN-pet]

straight droit [drwa]

  go straight on continuez tout droit [koNtee-nœ-ay too drwa]

  a straight whisky un whisky sec

straightaway immédiatement [eemayd-yat-mON]

strange *(odd)* bizarre

  (unknown) inconnu [ANkonœ]

stranger un inconnu [ANkonœ]

  (woman) une inconnue

  I'm a stranger here je ne suis pas d'ici [Juh nuh swee pa dee-see]

strawberry une fraise [frez]

street la rue [rœ]

street map un plan [plON]

string: have you got any string? est-ce que vous avez de la *ficelle*? [eskuh voo zavay duh la fee-sel]

stroke: he's had a stroke il a eu une attaque [eel ah ∞ ∞n atak]

strong fort [for]

stuck *(drawer etc)* bloqué [blokay]

student un étudiant [aytood-yON]
(female) une étudiante [aytood-yONT]

stupid stupide [stoopeed]

such: such a lot tant [tON]

suddenly tout d'un coup [too dAN koo]

sugar du sucre [sookr]

suit *(man's)* un complet [kON-pleh]
(woman's) un tailleur [tI-yur]

suitable convenable [kONvuh-nahbl]

suitcase une valise [valeez]

summer l'été [ay-tay]

sun le soleil [solay]
  in the sun au soleil [o...]
  out of the sun à l'abri du soleil [ah la-bree...]

sunbathe se faire bronzer [suh fair brON-zay]

sun block un écran total [aykrON toh-tahl]

sunburn un coup de soleil [koo duh solay]

sun cream une crème solaire [krem solair]

Sunday dimanche [dee-mONsh]

sunglasses des lunettes de soleil [loo-net duh solay]

sun lounger une chaise longue [shez lONg]

sunstroke une insolation [ANsolass-yON]

suntan le bronzage [brON-zahJ]

suntan oil de l'huile solaire [weel solair]

supermarket le supermarché [soopair-marshay]

sure: I'm not sure je ne suis pas sûr [Juh nuh swee pa soor]
  are you sure? vous êtes sûr? [voo zet...]

sure! bien entendu! [b-yAN ONtON-doo]

surfboard une planche de surf [plONsh duh surf]

surfing: to go surfing faire du surf [fair doo surf]

surname le nom de famille [nON duh fa-mee]

swearword un gros mot [gro mo]

sweat *(verb)* transpirer [trONspee-ray]

sweater un pull [pool]

sweet *(dessert)* un dessert [day-sair]

  it's too sweet c'est trop sucré [seh tro sookray]

sweets des bonbons [bONbON]

swerve: I had to swerve j'ai dû donner un coup de volant [Jay doo donay AN koo duh volON]

swim: I'm going for a swim je vais *me baigner* [Juh veh muh ben-yay]

  I can't swim je ne sais pas *nager* [Juh nuh seh pa na-Jay]

  let's go for a swim allons nous baigner [alON noo ben-yay]

swimming costume le maillot de bain [my-yo duh bAN]

swimming pool la piscine [pee-seen]

Swiss suisse [sweess]

  (man) le Suisse

  (woman) la Suissesse [sweess-ess]

switch l'interrupteur [ANtairooptur]

  to switch on allumer [aloomay]

  to switch off éteindre [aytANdr]

Switzerland la Suisse [sweess]

syndicat d'initiative tourist office

T [tay]

table une table [tahbl]

  a table for four une table pour quatre

table wine du vin de table [vAN duh tahbl]

taille size

take prendre [prONdr]

can I take this (with me)? est-ce que je peux emporter ça? [eskuh JUH puh ONportay sa]

will you take me to the airport? est-ce que vous pouvez m'emmener à l'aéroport? [eskuh vous poovay mONm-nay...]

how long will it take? combien de temps est-ce que ça prend? [kONb-yAN duh tON eskuh sa prON]

somebody has taken my bags quelqu'un a pris mes sacs [kelkAN ah pree...]

can I take you out tonight? est-ce que vous voulez sortir avec moi ce soir? [eskuh voo voolay sorteer ah-vek mwa suh swahr]

is this seat taken? est-ce que cette place est prise? [eskuh set plass eh preez]

I'll take it je le/la prends [JUH luh/la prON]

talk *(verb)* parler [parlay]

tall *(person)* grand [grON]

tampons des tampons hygiéniques [tONpON eeJ-yay-neek]

tan le bronzage [brON-zahJ]

  I want to get a tan je veux bronzer [JUH vuh brON-zay]

tank *(of car etc)* le réservoir [rayzair-vwahr]

tap le robinet [robeeneh]

tape *(cassette)* une cassette

tape-recorder un magnétophone [man-yayto-fon]

tariff le tarif [ta-reef]

taste le goût [goo]

  can I taste it? est-ce que je peux goûter? [eskuh JUH puh gootay]

taxi un taxi

  will you get me a taxi? est-ce que vous pouvez m'appeler un taxi? [eskuh voo poovay maplay...]

  where can I get a taxi? où est-ce que je peux trouver un taxi? [weskuh JUH puh troovay...]

taxi-driver le chauffeur de taxi

tea le thé [tay]

could I have a cup of tea? est-ce que je peux avoir un thé? [eskuh ʒuh puh avwahr...]
with milk/lemon au lait/citron [o leh/seetrON]

> *YOU MAY HEAR*
> une tasse ou une théière? *a cup or a pot?*

✈ Normally served without milk.

teach: could you teach me some French? est-ce que vous pouvez m'apprendre quelques mots de français? [eskuh voo poovay maprONdr kelkuh mo duh frON-seh]
teacher le/la professeur [professur]
(primary) l'instituteur [ANsteetootur]
(woman) l'institutrice [ANsteetootreess]
telephone le téléphone [taylay-fon]
go to **phone**
telephone directory l'annuaire téléphonique [annoo-air taylayfoneek]
television la télévision [taylay-veez-yON]
I'd like to watch television j'aimerais regarder la télévision [ʒemreh ruhgar-day...]
tell: could you tell me where...? est-ce que vous pouvez me *dire* où...? [eskuh voo poovay muh deer oo]
could you tell him...? pourriez-vous lui dire que...? [pooree-ay-voo lwee deer kuh]
I told him that... je lui ai dit que... [ʒuh lwee ay dee kuh]
temperature *(weather etc)* la température [tONpay-ra-toor]
he's got a temperature il a de la fièvre [...fee-evr]
tennis le tennis [tay-neess]
tennis ball une balle de tennis [bal duh tay-neess]
tennis court un court de tennis [koor duh tay-neess]
tennis racket une raquette de tennis [ra-ket duh

tay-neess]
tent la tente [tONT]
terminus le terminus [tairmeenœss]
terrible affreux [afruh]

> The French word **terrible** can mean both 'terrible' and 'fantastic'.

terrific fantastique [fONtasteek]
tête de station taxi rank
text: I'll text you je vous enverrai un texto [Juh voo zONvairay...]
  (familiar) je t'enverrai un texto
than que [kuh]
  bigger than... plus grand que... [...kuh]
thanks, thank you merci [mair-see]
  thank you very much merci beaucoup [...bo-koo]
  no thank you non merci [nON...]
  thank you for your help merci de votre aide [...duh...]

> *YOU MAY THEN HEAR*
> je vous en prie *or* de rien *you're welcome*

that ce/cette [suh/set]
  that man/that table ce monsieur/cette table
  I would like that one j'aimerais celui-là/celle-là [...suh-lwee-la/sel-la]
  how do you pronounce that? comment ça se prononce? [komON sa suh prononss]
  and that? et ça? [ay sa]
  I think that... je crois que... [...kuh]
the le/la [luh/la]
  (plural) les [lay]

> **Le** and **la** change to **l'** in front a word starting with a vowel.
>   **the airport** l'aéroport

theatre le théâtre [tay-ahtr]
their leur [lur]
  their hotel leur hôtel
  their children leurs enfants
theirs le/la leur [luh/la lur]
  it's theirs c'est à eux [seh ta uh]
  (belonging to women) c'est à elles [...el]
them: I've lost them je *les* ai perdus [Juh lay zay pairdoo]
  I gave it to them je le *leur* ai donné [...lur...]
  with/for them avec/pour eux [...uh]
  (with/for women) avec/pour elles [...el]
  who? – them qui? – eux/elles
then *(at that time)* alors [alor]
  (after that) ensuite [ON-sweet]
there là [la]
  how do I get there? comment est-ce qu'on y va? [komON eskON nee va]
  is there/are there...? est-ce qu'il y a...? [eskeel-ya]
  there is/there are... il y a.... [eelya]
  there isn't/there aren't... il n'y a pas de... [eel n-ya pa duh]
  there you are *(giving something)* voilà [vwa-la]
these ces [say]
  these apples ces pommes [say...]
  can I take these? est-ce que je peux prendre ceux-ci/celles-ci? [...suh-see/sel-see]
they ils/elles [eel/el]

> Use **elles** not just for women but for all nouns with **la** or **une**.

thick épais [ay-peh]
  (stupid) bête [bet]
thief un voleur [volur]
  (woman) une voleuse [volurz]
thigh la cuisse [kweess]

thin mince [mANss]

thing une chose [shohz]

  I've lost all my things j'ai perdu toutes mes affaires [Jay pairdoo toot may zafair]

think penser [poNsay]

  I'll think it over je vais y réfléchir [Juh veh zee rayflay-sheer]

  I think so je crois [Juh krwa]

  I don't think so je ne crois pas [...pa]

third *(adjective)* troisième [trwahz-yem]

thirsty: I'm thirsty j'ai soif [Jay swahf]

this ce/cette [suh/set]

  this man/table ce monsieur/cette table

  can I have this one? j'aimerais celui-ci/celle-ci [suh-lwee-see/sel-see]

  this is... c'est... [seh]

  this is very good c'est très bon [seh treh...]

  this is my wife/this is Mr... *(introducing)* je vous présente ma femme/Monsieur... [Juh voo pray-zONt...]

  is this...? est-ce que c'est...? [eskuh seh]

  and this? et ça? [ay sa]

those ces [say]

  those apples ces pommes

  can I take those? est-ce que je peux prendre ceux-là/celles-là? [...suh-la/sel-la]

  no, not these, those non, pas ceux-ci, ceux-là

thread du fil [feel]

throat la gorge [gorJ]

throttle l'accélérateur [axay-lay-ra-tur]

through *(across)* à travers [ah tra-vair]

  to go through Orléans passer par Orléans [pa-say...]

  it's through there c'est par là [seh...]

throw lancer [loN-say]

thumb le pouce [pooss]

thunder le tonnerre [tonair]

thunderstorm un orage [orahJ]
Thursday jeudi [Juh-dee]
ticket *(plane, train, show)* le billet [bee-yeh]
  (bus, metro, cloakroom) le ticket [teekeh]
tie *(necktie)* une cravate [kra-vat]
tight *(clothes)* juste [Jœst]
tights un collant [kolonN]
time le temps [tonN]
  I haven't got time je n'ai pas le temps [Juh nay pa luh tonN]
  for the time being pour le moment [...momonN]
  this time/last time/next time cette fois/la dernière fois/la prochaine fois [set fwa/la dairn-yair.../proshen...]
  three times trois fois
  have a good time! amusez-vous bien! [amœ-zay voo b-yanN]
  what's the time? quelle heure il est? [kel ur eel eh]

HOW TO TELL THE TIME
  it's one o'clock il est une heure [eeleh œn ur]
  it's two/three/four o'clock il est deux/trois/quatre heures [duh/trwa/katr ur]
  it's 5/10/20/25 past seven il est sept heures cinq/dix/vingt/vingt-cinq [...set ur sanNk/deess/vanN/vanNt-sanNk]
  it's quarter past eight/eight fifteen il est huit heures et quart [...ay kar]
  it's half past nine/nine thirty il est neuf heures et demie/neuf heures trente [...duh-mee]
  it's 25/20/10/5 to ten il est dix heures moins vingt-cinq/vingt/dix/cinq [...mwanN...]
  it's quarter to eleven/10.45 il est onze
---

heures moins le quart
it's twelve o'clock (am/pm) il est midi/
minuit [...meedee/meen-wee]
at one o'clock à une heure
at three thirty à trois heures et demie

The 24-hour clock is commonly used in
spoken French. So, in the evening, instead
of
  it's seven pm il est sept heures du soir

you could say
  il est dix-neuf heures

Don't use **demi** or **quart** with the 24-hour
clock
  it's seven fifteen/thirty pm il est dix-
neuf heures quinze/trente

timetable un horaire [o-rair]
tin *(can)* une boîte [bwat]
tin-opener un ouvre-boîte [oovruh-bwat]
tip un pourboire [poor-bwahr]
  is the tip included? est-ce que le pourboire est
compris? [eskuh luh...eh koNpree]

✈ Tip taxi drivers and lavatory attendants.
  In bars and restaurants service is always
  included and you should see **service
  compris** on the bill. French people don't
  normally leave a tip.

tired fatigué [fatee-gay]
  I'm tired je suis fatigué [Juh swee...]
tirez pull
tissues des Kleenex®
to à [ah]
  to Cherbourg à Cherbourg
  to England en Angleterre [ON...]

to Pierre's chez Pierre [shay...]
go to **time**

> When **à** is used with **le** it becomes **au**.
> With the plural **les** it becomes **aux**.
>   **to the United States** aux États-Unis

toast *(piece of)* du pain grillé [pAN gree-yay]

> **Un toast** is a toasted sandwich.

tobacco du tabac [ta-ba]
today aujourd'hui [oJoordwee]
toe le doigt de pied [dwa duh p-yay]
together ensemble [ON-sONbl]
  we're together nous sommes ensemble
  can we pay all together? est-ce que nous
  pouvons payer tous ensemble? [eskuh noo
  poovON pay-yay tooss...]
toilet les toilettes [twa-let]
  where are the toilets? où sont les toilettes? [oo
  sON lay...]
  I have to go to the toilet il faut que j'aille aux
  toilettes [eel fo kuh Ja-ee o...]

> ✈ You can use the toilet in cafés or bars but
> the bar staff would appreciate your buying
> something first. There are also coin-oper-
> ated toilet cabins on the street in the bigger
> cities.

toilet paper: there's no toilet paper il n'y a pas
de *papier hygiénique* [eel n-ya pa duh pap-yay
eeJ-yay-neek]
tomato une tomate [tomat]
tomato juice un jus de tomate [Joo duh tomat]
tomato ketchup le ketchup
tomorrow demain [duh-mAN]
  tomorrow morning demain matin [...matAN]
  tomorrow afternoon demain après-midi

[...apreh-mee-dee]
  tomorrow evening demain soir [...swahr]
  the day after tomorrow après-demain
  [apreh-...]
  see you tomorrow à demain
tongue la langue [lONg]
tonic (water) un schweppes® [shweps]
tonight ce soir [suh swahr]
tonsillitis une angine [ON-Jeen]
too trop [tro]
  (also) aussi [o-see]
  that's too much c'est trop [seh...]
  me too moi aussi [mwa o-see]
tool un outil [oo-tee]
tooth une dent [dON]
toothache: I've got toothache j'ai mal aux
  dents [Jay mal o dON]
toothbrush une brosse à dents [bross ah dON]
toothpaste du dentifrice [dONtee-freess]
top: on top of sur [soor]
  on the top floor au dernier étage [o dairn-yay
  ray-tahJ]
  at the top en haut [ON o]
torch une lampe de poche [lONp duh posh]
total le total [toh-tal]
tough dur [door]
tour une excursion [exkoorss-yON]
  (of area) un circuit [seer-kwee]
  (of town, castle etc) une visite guidée [veezeet
  gheeday]
  we'd like to go on a tour of... nous aimerions
  visiter... [noo zemuh-ree-yON veezee-tay]
  we're touring around nous visitons la région
  [noo veezee-tON la rayJ-yON]
tourist un/une touriste [tooreest]
  I'm a tourist je suis un/une touriste
tourist office l'office de tourisme [ofeess duh

tooreess-muh]

toutes directions through traffic

tow remorquer [ruh-morkay]
  can you give me a tow? est-ce que vous
  pouvez me remorquer? [eskuh voo poovay
  muh...]

towards vers [vair]
  he was coming straight towards me il venait
  droit vers moi [eel vuhneh drwa vair mwa]

towel une serviette [sairv-yet]

town une ville [veel]
  in town en ville [ON...]
  would you take me into town? est-ce que
  vous pouvez m'emmener en ville? [eskuh voo
  poovay mONm-nay...]

towrope une corde de dépannage [kord duh
daypanahJ]

traditional traditionnel [tradeess-yonel]
  a traditional French meal un repas
  typiquement français [ruhpa teepeekmON frON-
  seh]

traffic la circulation [seerkoo-lass-yON]

traffic jam un embouteillage [ONbootay-ahJ]

traffic lights les feux [fuh]

train le train [trAN]

> ✈ Remember to punch your ticket before
> boarding the train: look for orange-col-
> oured machines located on platforms or for
> the notice **compostez votre billet.**

trainers des baskets [bass-ket]

train station la gare [gar]

traiteur delicatessen; caterers

tranquillizers des calmants [kalmON]

translate traduire [tradweer]
  would you translate that for me? est-ce que
  vous pouvez me traduire ça? [eskuh voo poovay

muh...sa]
travaux roadworks
travel voyager [vwy-ahJay]
travel agent's une agence de voyage [ah-JONss duh vwy-ahJ]
traveller's cheque un 'traveller's cheque'
tree un arbre [arbr]
tremendous *(very good)* formidable [formeedahbl]
trim: just a trim, please coupez juste un peu, s'il vous plaît [koopay Joost AN puh...]
trip *(journey)* un voyage [vwy-ahJ]
(outing) une excursion [exkoorss-yON]
we want to go on a trip to... nous voulons faire une excursion à... [noo voolON fair oon...]
trouble des ennuis [ON-nwee]
I'm having trouble with... j'ai des ennuis avec... [Jay day...]
trousers le pantalon [pONta-lON]
true vrai [vreh]
it's not true c'est pas vrai [seh pa...]
trunks *(swimming)* le slip de bain [...duh bAN]
try essayer [esay-yay]
can I try it on? est-ce que je peux l'essayer? [eskuh Juh puh...]
T-shirt un 'T-shirt'
t.t.c., toutes taxes comprises inclusive of tax
Tuesday mardi [mardee]
tunnel un tunnel [too-nel]
turn: where do we turn off? où est-ce qu'il faut tourner? [weskeel fo toornay]
T.V.A. VAT
twice deux fois [duh fwa]
twice as much deux fois plus [...plooss]
twin beds des lits jumeaux [lee Joomo]
twin room une chambre à deux lits [shONbr ah duh lee]
typical typique [tee-peek]

tyre un pneu [pnuh]
  I need a new tyre il me faut un pneu neuf [eel muh fo AN pnuh nurf]

✈ lb/sq in	18	20	22	26	28	30
kg/sq cm	1.3	1.4	1.5	1.7	2	2.1

U [∞]

ugly laid [leh]
ulcer un ulcère [∞l-sair]
umbrella un parapluie [para-plwee]
uncle: my uncle mon oncle [MON ONkl]
uncomfortable inconfortable [ANKON-for-tahbl]
unconscious: he's unconscious il a perdu connaissance [eel ah pairdoo koneh-SONss]
under sous [soo]
underdone pas assez cuit [pa zassay kwee]
underground *(rail)* le métro [maytro]
understand: I understand je comprends [Juh KONproN]
  I don't understand je ne comprends pas [Juh nuh...pa]
  do you understand? est-ce que vous comprenez? [eskuh voo KONpruh-nay]
undo défaire [day-fair]
unfriendly désagréable [dayz-agray-ahbl]
unhappy malheureux [malur-ruh]
United States les États-Unis [ayta-zoo-nee]
university l'université [∞nee-vairseetay]
unleaded le sans plomb [SON plON]
unlock ouvrir [oovreer]
until jusqu'à [Jooska]
  not until Tuesday pas avant mardi [pa zavON mardee]
unusual inhabituel [eenabee-too-el]
up en haut [ON o]

up there là-haut [la-o]

he's not up yet il n'est pas encore levé [eel neh pa zON-kor luh-vay]

what's up? que se passe-t-il? [kuh suh pasteel]

upside-down à l'envers [ah lON-vair]

upstairs en haut [ON o]

urgent urgent [œr-JON]

us: can you help us? est-ce que vous pouvez *nous* aider? [eskuh voo poovay noo zay-day]

  with/for us avec/pour nous

  it's us c'est nous

  who? – us qui? – nous

USA les USA [œ-ess-ah]

use: can I use...? est-ce que je peux utiliser...? [eskuh Juh puh œteelee-zay]

useful utile [œteel]

usual habituel [abee-tœ-el]

  as usual comme d'habitude [kom dabee-tœd]

usually d'habitude [dabee-tœd]

U-turn un demi-tour [duh-mee-toor]

V [vay]

---

vacate *(room)* libérer [leebay-ray]

vacation les vacances [vakONss]

vaccination un vaccin [vak-sAN]

vacuum flask un thermos [tairmoss]

valid valable [valahbl]

  how long is it valid for? c'est valable combien de temps? [seh...kONb-yAN duh tON]

valley la vallée [valay]

valuable de valeur [duh valur]

  will you look after my valuables? est-ce que vous pouvez me garder mes objets de valeur? [eskuh voo poovay muh garday may zob-Jeh...]

value la valeur [valur]

van une camionnette [kam-yonet]

vanilla la vanille [va-nee]
veal du veau [vo]
vegetables des légumes [lay-gœm]
vegetarian végétarien [vayJay-taree-AN]
vendre: à vendre for sale
ventilator le ventilateur [vONtee-la-tur]
very très [treh]
  very much beaucoup [bo-koo]
via par
village un village [vee-lahJ]
vine une vigne [veen-yuh]
vinegar du vinaigre [vee-negr]
vineyard un vignoble [veen-yobl]
violent violent [veeolON]
virages bends
visit *(verb)* visiter [veezee-tay]
vitesse limitée à... speed limit...
vodka une vodka
voice la voix [vwa]
voie 6 platform 6
voltage le voltage [voltahJ]

  ✈ 220 as in the UK.

vous n'avez pas la priorité give way

W [doobluh-vay]

waist la taille [tɪ]
wait: will we have to wait long? est-ce qu'il
  faudra *attendre* longtemps? [eskeel fo-dra atONdr
  lON-tON]
  wait for me attendez-moi! [atON-day-mwa]
  I'm waiting for a friend/my wife j'attends un
  ami/ma femme [JatON...]
waiter le serveur [sair-vur]
  waiter! s'il vous plaît! [seel voo pleh]
waitress la serveuse [sair-vurz]

wake: will you wake me up at 7.30? est-ce que vous pouvez me *réveiller* à 7.30? [eskuh voo poovay muh rayvay-yay...]

Wales le Pays de Galles [payee duh gal]

walk: can we walk there? est-ce qu'on peut y *aller à pied*? [eskON puh ee alay ah p-yay]

walking shoes des chaussures de marche [sho-soor duh marsh]

wall le mur [moor]

wallet le portefeuille [port-fuh-ee]

want: I want... je veux... [Juh vuh]

I want to talk to... je veux parler à...

what do you want? qu'est-ce que vous voulez/ tu veux? *(polite/familiar)* [keskuh voo voolay/too vuh]

I don't want to je ne veux pas [Juh nuh vuh pa]

he/she wants to... il/elle veut... [eel vuh]

war la guerre [gair]

warm chaud [sho]

warning un avertissement [avairteess-mON]

was

> Here is the past tense of the verb 'to be'.
>
> **I was** j'étais [Jayteh]
> **you were** *(familiar)* tu étais [too ayteh]
> **you were** *(polite)* vous étiez [voo zaytee-ay]
> **he/she/it was** il/elle était [eel/el ayteh]
> **it was** c'était [sayteh]
> **we were** nous étions [noo zaytee-ON]
> **you were** *(plural)* vous étiez
> **they were** ils/elles étaient [eel/el zayteh]

wash: can you wash these for me? est-ce que vous pouvez me *laver* ceci? [eskuh voo poovay muh lavay suh-see]

washbasin un lavabo

washer *(for nut)* un joint [JWAN]

washing machine une machine à laver [...ah lavay]

washing powder de la lessive en poudre [lesseev ON poodr]

wasp une guêpe [gep]

watch *(wristwatch)* une montre [mONtr]

  will you watch my bags for me? est-ce que vous pouvez *surveiller* mes bagages? [eskuh voo poovay sœr-vay-yay may bagahJ]

  watch out! attention! [ah-tONss-yON]

water l'eau [o]

  can I have some water? est-ce que je peux avoir de l'eau? [eskuh Juh puh avwahr...]

  hot and cold running water eau courante chaude et froide [o koo-rONt shohd ay frwahd]

waterfall la chute d'eau [shœt doh]

waterproof imperméable [ANpair-may-ahbl]

waterskiing le ski nautique [skee no-teek]

way: it's this way c'est par ici [seh par ee-see]

  it's that way c'est par là [..la]

  do it this way faites comme ceci [fet kom suh-see]

  no way! pas question! [pa kest-yON]

  is it on the way to...? est-ce sur la route de...? [ess sœr la root duh]

  could you tell me the way to get to...? pouvez-vous m'indiquer le chemin pour aller à...? [poovay-voo mANdeekay luh shuh-mAN poor alay ah]

  go to **where** *for answers*

we nous [noo]

weak faible [febl]

weather le temps [tON]

  what filthy weather! quel sale temps! [kel sal...]

  what's the weather forecast? quelles sont les prévisions de la météo? [kel sON lay prayveez-yON duh la maytay-o]

> *YOU MAY THEN HEAR*
> couvert *overcast*
> du soleil *sunny*
> de la pluie *rain*
> très froid *very cold*
> très chaud *very hot*

website un site Internet [seet ANtairnet]

Wednesday mercredi [mairkruh-dee]

week une semaine [suh-men]
  a week today dans huit jours [dON wee JOor]
  a week tomorrow demain en huit [duh-mAN ON weet]

weekend: at the weekend ce 'week-end' [suh...]

weight le poids [pwa]

welcome: you're welcome je vous en prie [Juh voo zON pree]

well: I'm not feeling well je ne me sens pas très bien [Juh nuh muh sON pa treh b-yAN]
  he's not well il ne va pas bien [eel nuh va pa b-yAN]
  how are you? – very well, thanks comment allez-vous? – très bien, merci [komON talay voo – treh b-yAN mair-see]
  you speak English very well vous parlez très bien anglais [voo parlay...]
  well, well! *(surprise)* tiens! [t-yAN]

Welsh gallois/galloise [gal-wa/gal-waz]

were *go to* **was**

west l'ouest [oo-est]

West Indies les Antilles [ON-tee]

wet mouillé [moo-yay]
  it's so wet here il pleut tout le temps ici [eel pluh too luh tON ee-see]

wet suit une combinaison de plongée [kONbee-nezzON duh plON-Jay]

what? quoi? [kwa]

what is that? qu'est-ce que c'est? [keskuh seh]
what did she say? qu'est-ce qu'elle a dit?
[keskel ah dee]
what for? pourquoi? [poor-kwa]
what train? quel train? [kel...]
wheel la roue [roo]
wheel chair un fauteuil roulant [fo-tuh-ee roo-lON]
when? quand? [kON]
  when is breakfast? à quelle heure est le petit
déjeuner? [ah kel ur...]
where? où? [oo]
  where is...? où est...? [oo eh]

> *YOU MAY THEN HEAR*
> à droite/gauche *on/to the right/left*
> tournez *turn*
> prenez *take*
> continuez tout droit *keep straight on*
> jusqu'au... *until the...*
> aux feux *at the lights*

which? quel/quelle [kel]
  which one? lequel/laquelle? [luh-kel/la-kel]

> *YOU MAY THEN HEAR*
> celui-ci/celle-ci *this one*
> celui-là/celle-là *that one*

whisky un whisky
white blanc [blON]
white wine un vin blanc [vAN blON]
Whitsun la Pentecôte [pONt-kot]
who? qui? [kee]
whose: whose is this? *à qui* est ceci? [ah kee eh
suh-see]

> *YOU MAY THEN HEAR*
> c'est à moi *it's mine*
> c'est à lui/eux *it's his/theirs*

why? pourquoi? [poor-kwa]
  why not? pourquoi pas? [...pa]

> *YOU MAY THEN HEAR*
> parce que... *because...*

wide large [larJ]
wife: my wife ma femme [...fam]
will: when will it be finished? quand est-ce que
ça sera terminé? [kON teskuh sa suhra tairmeenay]
  will you do it? est-ce que vous pouvez le faire?
[eskuh voo poovay luh fair?]
  I'll come back je reviendrai [Juh ruhv-yANdray]
win gagner [gan-yay]
  who won? qui a gagné? [kee ah gan-yay]
wind le vent [VON]
window la fenêtre [fuh-netr]
  (of car) la vitre [veetr]
  (of shop) la vitrine [veetreen]
  near the window près de la fenêtre [preh
duh...]
window seat une place côté fenêtre [plass ko-tay
fuh-netr]
windscreen le pare-brise [par-breez]
windscreen wipers les essuie-glaces [eswee glass]
windy: it's too windy il y a trop de vent [eelya
tro duh VON]
wine du vin [VAN]
  can I see the wine list? est-ce je peux avoir la
carte des vins? [eskuh JuH puh avwahr la kart day
VAN]
  two red/white wines please deux verres de
vin rouge/blanc, s'il vous plaît [duh vair duh VAN
rooJ/blON...]

> ✈ There are so many to choose from and you
> won't go wrong with a **vin ordinaire** or a
> local wine (**vin de pays**).

Some wine words:
dry sec
sweet doux [doo]
medium demi-sec
sparkling mousseux [moossuh]

winter l'hiver [ee-vair]
wire du fil métallique [feel maytaleek]
  (electric) le fil électrique [...aylek-treek]
wish: best wishes meilleurs vœux [may-yur vuh]
  (on letter) amitiés [ameet-yay]
with avec [ah-vek]
without sans [sON]
witness un témoin [tay-mwAN]
  will you act as a witness for me? est-ce que
  vous pouvez me servir de témoin? [eskuh voo
  poovay muh sair-veer...]
woman une femme [fam]
  women les femmes [fam]
wonderful magnifique [man-yee-feek]
won't: the car won't start la voiture ne démarre
  pas [...nuh day-mar pa]
wood le bois [bwa]
wool de la laine [len]
word un mot [mo]
  I don't know that word je ne connais pas ce
  mot [Juh nuh koneh pa suh mo]
work travailler [travI-yay]
  I work in London je travaille à Londres [Juh
  travI...]
  it's not working ça ne marche pas [san marsh pa]
worry: I'm worried about him je suis inquiet/
  inquiète pour lui [Juh swee zANk-yeh/zANk-yet
  poor lwee]
  don't worry ne vous inquiétez pas [nuh voo
  zANk-yay-tay pa]
worse: it's worse c'est pire [seh peer]

worst le/la pire [peer]

worth: it's not worth that much ça ne vaut pas autant [sa nuh vo pa o-toN]

worthwhile: is it worthwhile going to...? est-ce que ça vaut la peine d'aller à...? [eskuh sa vo la pen dalay ah]

wrap: could you wrap it up? est-ce que vous pouvez me l'envelopper? [eskuh voo poovay muh loNv-lopay]

wrench *(tool)* une clé anglaise [klay oN-glez]

wrist le poignet [pwan-yeh]

write écrire [ay-kreer]

   could you write it down? est-ce que vous pouvez me l'écrire? [eskuh voo poovay muh...]

   I'll write to you je vous écrirai [juh voo zaykree-ray]

writing paper du papier à lettres [pap-yay ah letr]

wrong faux/fausse [fo/fohss]

   I think the bill's wrong je crois qu'il y a une erreur dans l'addition [juh krwa keelya oon air-rur doN ladeess-yoN]

   there's something wrong with... il y a des problèmes avec... [eelya day prob-lem...]

   you're wrong vous vous trompez [voo voo troN-pay]

   that's the wrong key ce n'est pas la bonne clef [suh neh pa la bon klay]

   sorry, wrong number *(I've got)* excusez-moi, j'ai fait un faux numéro [exkoo-zay mwa jay feh aN fo noomay-ro]

   (you've got) je crois que vous avez fait un faux numéro [juh krwa kuh...]

   I got the wrong train je me suis trompé de train [juh muh swee troNpay duh troN]

   what's wrong? qu'y a-t-il? [k-yateel]

Y [eegrek]

yacht un yacht [yot]
yard

> ✈ 1 yard = 91.44 cms = 0.91 m

year une année [anay]
  this year cette année [set...]
  next year l'année prochaine [...proshen]
yellow jaune [Jo-n]
yellow pages les pages jaunes [pahJ John]
yes oui [wee]

> To disagree with a statement containing a
> 'not' use **si**.
>   **you can't – yes, I can** tu ne peux pas –
>   mais si je peux

yesterday hier [yair]
  the day before yesterday avant-hier [ah-VONT-
  yair]
  yesterday morning hier matin [...matAN]
  yesterday afternoon hier après-midi [...apreh-
  mee-dee]
yet: is it ready yet? est-ce que c'est *déjà* prêt?
  [eskuh seh day-Ja preh]
  not yet pas encore [pa zON-kor]
yoghurt un yaourt [ya-oort]
you vous [voo]
  I don't understand you je ne vous comprends
  pas
  I'll send it to you je vous l'enverrai
  with/for you avec/pour vous
  is that you? c'est vous? [seh...]

> If you are talking to friends, casual
> acquaintances of your own age-group or
> children, you can use the familiar word for

'you' **tu** [too]. But you shouldn't use this form with people like bus drivers, shop assistants, hotel receptionists etc.
you are... tu es...
I don't understand you je ne *te* comprends pas [...tuh...]
I'll send it to you je te l'enverrai
with/for you avec/pour toi [...twa]
who? – you qui? – toi

young jeune [Jurn]
your votre [votr]
(with plural nouns) vos [vo]
(familiar) ton/ta [tON...]
(familiar plural) tes [tay]

Use **ton** or **ta** depending on whether the word following takes **le** or **la**.
your bag ton sac
your suitcase ta valise

yours le/la vôtre [luh/la vohtr]
(with plural nouns) les vôtres [lay vohtr]
(familiar) le tien/la tienne [luh t-yAN/la t-yen]
(familiar plural) les tiens/les tiennes [lay t-yAN/lay t-yen]
is this yours? c'est à vous/toi? [seh ta voo/twa]
youth hostel une auberge de jeunesse [o-bairJ duh Juh-ness]

Z [zed]

zero zéro [zayro]
below zero en dessous de zéro [ON duh-soo...]
zip une fermeture éclair [fairmuh-toor ay-klair]
could you put a new zip on? pourriez-vous changer la fermeture éclair? [pooree-ay-voo shONJay...]

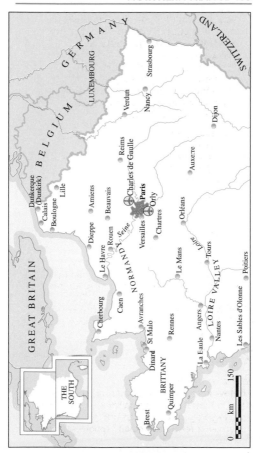

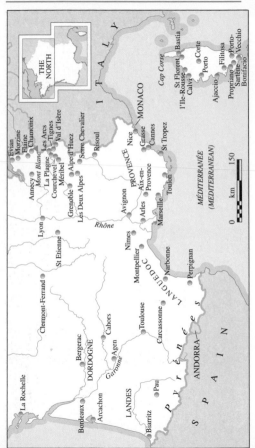

THE NORTH

I T A L Y

Cap Corse

Bastia
St Florent
l'Ile-Rousse
Calvi
Porto
Corte
Filitosa
Ajaccio
Propriano
Porto-
Vecchio
Sartène
Bonifacio

Évian
Morzine
Flaine
Chamonix
Mont Blanc
Les Arcs
La Plagne
Tignes
Courchevel
Val d'Isère
Méribel
Alpe d'Huez
Serre Chevalier
Risoul

MONACO
Nice
Grasse
Cannes
St Tropez

Annecy
Grenoble
Les Deux Alpes
PROVENCE
Aix-en-
Provence
Toulon

Lyon
Rhône
Avignon
Arles
Marseille

St Etienne
Nîmes
Montpellier
Narbonne
Perpignan

MÉDITERRANÉE
(MEDITERRANEAN)

0   km   150

Clermont-Ferrand
LANGUEDOC

Bergerac
Cahors
Toulouse
Carcassonne

La Rochelle
DORDOGNE
Agen
Garonne

Bordeaux
Arcachon
LANDES
Pau
ANDORRA

Biarritz
P y r é n é e s
S P A I N

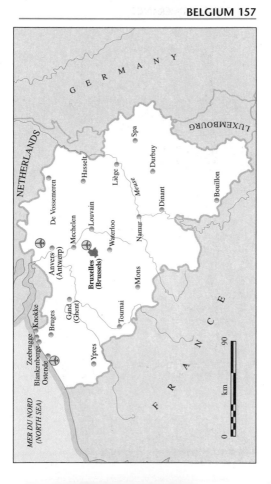

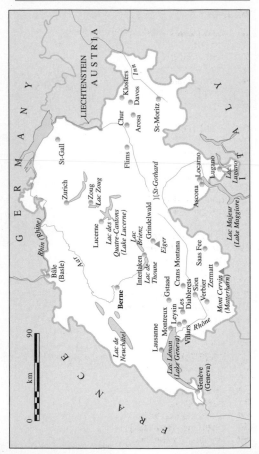

Numbers

0	zéro	[zayro]
1	un	[AN]
2	deux	[duh]
3	trois	[trwa]
4	quatre	[katr]
5	cinq	[sANk]
6	six	[seess]
7	sept	[set]
8	huit	[weet]
9	neuf	[nurf]
10	dix	[deess]
11	onze	[ONz]
12	douze	[dooz]
13	treize	[trez]
14	quatorze	[katorz]
15	quinze	[kANz]
16	seize	[sez]
17	dix-sept	[dee-set]
18	dix-huit	[deez-weet]
19	dix-neuf	[deez-nurf]
20	vingt	[vAN]
21	vingt-et-un	[vAN-tay-AN]
22	vingt-deux	[vANt-duh]
23	vingt-trois	[vANt-trwa]
24	vingt-quatre	
25	vingt-cinq	
26	vingt-six	
27	vingt-sept	
28	vingt-huit	
29	vingt-neuf	
30	trente	[trONt]
31	trente-et-un	
40	quarante	[karONt]
50	cinquante	[sAN-kONt]
60	soixante	[swa-sONt]

70	soixante-dix [swa-sONt-deess]
71	soixante-et-onze [swa-sON tay ONz]
72	soixante-douze
73	soixante-treize
79	soixante-dix-neuf
80	quatre-vingts [katr-vAN]
81	quatre-vingt-un
90	quatre-vingt-dix
91	quatre-vingt-onze
100	cent [sON]
101	cent un [sON AN]
165	cent soixante-cinq
200	deux cents [duh sON]
300	trois cents
400	quatre cents
1,000	mille [meel]
2,000	deux mille
4,653	quatre mille six cent cinquante-trois
1,000,000	un million [meel-yON]

In Switzerland and Belgium also:

70	septante [septONt]
80	huitante [weetONt]
90	nonante [nonONt]
71	septante et un
85	huitante cinq
99	nonante neuf

NB In French a comma is used for a decimal point; for thousands you usually use a space, eg 3 000

The alphabet: how to spell in French

a [ah] **b** [bay] **c** [say] **d** [day] **e** [uh] **f** [ef] **g** [jay]
h [ash] **i** [ee] **j** [Jee] **k** [ka] **l** [el] **m** [em] **n** [en]
o [o] **p** [pay] **q** [koo] **r** [air] **s** [ess] **t** [tay] **u** [oo]
v [vay] **w** [doobluh-vay] **x** [eeks] **y** [eegrek]
z [zed]